Six
Simple
Rules

Six Simple Rules

How to Manage Complexity without Getting Complicated

YVES MORIEUX
PETER TOLLMAN

HARVARD BUSINESS REVIEW PRESS

BOSTON, MASSACHUSETTS

The web addresses referenced in this book were live and correct at the
time of the book's publication but may be subject to change.

Library of Congress Cataloging-in-Publication Data

Morieux, Yves, 1960-
  Six simple rules : how to manage complexity without getting
  complicated / Yves Morieux, Peter Tollman.
     pages cm
  ISBN 978-1-4221-9055-5 (alk. paper)
1. Complex organizations—Management. 2. Organizational effectiveness.
3. Organizational behavior. 4. Management. I. Tollman, Peter. II. Title.
  HD31.M6292 2014
  658—dc23

                          2013045502

The paper used in this publication meets the requirements of the
American National Standard for Permanence of Paper for Publications
and Documents in Libraries and Archives Z39.48-1992.

Contents

Six
Simple
Rules

Introduction

Why Managers Need the
Six Simple Rules

How do companies create value and achieve competitive advantage in an age of great complexity? This is a question we constantly ask ourselves as we go about our work of helping chief executives and their leadership teams build successful businesses.

When we reflect on our work with the companies we have helped over the years—five hundred or more in all kinds of industries in more than forty countries—what we remember most vividly is rarely the specific problem that caused a business leader to call us in. Rather what comes to mind is the people—an airline maintenance worker, a head of R&D, a hotel receptionist, a sales director, a train driver, a CEO—all of whom were facing more or less the same situation. They confronted a challenge that seemed impossible: increased complexity in their business. We'll discuss complexity in greater detail further along, but briefly, we mean that companies face an increasing number of performance requirements; the number can be in the range of twenty-five to forty different requirements, far more than twenty or even ten years ago. Often the requirements are contradictory in nature, such as the need to produce goods of high quality that can sell at low prices, or for services to be globally consistent yet also responsive to local demands (see the sidebar "The Complexity Challenge and Opportunity").

To meet the challenges of complexity, the people we remember so well had tried applying the "best" management thinking and following the "best practices" of the day—including, as we'll see, both structural fixes and people-oriented approaches—and those practices had failed to bring them success in their efforts in creating value. They were working hard and, when they failed to achieve the results they wanted, they worked harder. But they didn't have much hope the outcome would be any different. They felt overwhelmed, trapped, and often misunderstood and unsupported by their teams, bosses, and boards.

What's striking is how poorly served these people were by the conventional wisdom in management—the management theories, models, and practices developed over the past one hundred years. Instead of helping these people manage the growing complexity of business, all the supposed solutions only seemed to make things worse. There had to be a better way, and through on-the-ground work with these people and their organizations, we have battle tested the approach that we describe in this book. We call this approach *smart simplicity* and it hinges on the six simple rules.[1]

Yves comes at the issue as director of the Institute for Organization at The Boston Consulting Group (BCG), where he brings economics and social sciences to bear on the strategic and organizational challenges of companies and their executive teams—especially as they relate to complexity. Yves formulated the smart simplicity approach to managing complexity, based on his background in research and theoretical inquiry, as well as his extensive work with clients in the United States, Europe, and Asia-Pacific. As head of the firm's People and Organization Practice in North America, Peter has partnered with Yves to implement the six rules of the smart simplicity approach, drawing on his long experience working with some of the world's most prominent companies.

Through our client work and continued research, we have continuously refined the rules so that they offer a theoretical framework and a set of practicable management tools. We are actively working together, and with our BCG colleagues, to successfully apply the simple rules—helping companies around the world grow, create enduring value, and achieve competitive advantage.

How Complexity Leads to Complicatedness

To understand the power of the simple rules and why they are so essential in business, let's start by defining the problem. Today, companies have to deal with greater business complexity than ever before. This complexity arises from the requirements companies must meet to create value for their stakeholders. These

THE COMPLEXITY CHALLENGE AND OPPORTUNITY

Performing on Everything for Everyone

The BCG Institute for Organization created the Complexity Index by tracking the evolution of the number of performance requirements at a representative sample of companies in the United States and Europe over a period of fifty-five years—from 1955 (the year the *Fortune* 500 list was created) through 2010. In 1955, companies typically committed to between four and seven performance imperatives; today they commit to between twenty-five and forty.

Between 15 percent and 50 percent of those performance requirements are contradictory. Around 1955, hardly any were. Companies currently may have to offer high-quality products and sell them at rock-bottom prices; goods have to be innovative and also produced efficiently; supply chains must be fast and reliable; service must be globally consistent and, at the same time, highly responsive locally. When a company is able to reconcile valuable yet contradictory requirements, it breaks a compromise and, in so doing, unleashes new value for customers. This new value creates advantage and fuels profitable growth.

We see two important causes for the growth of complexity. First, shifting trade barriers and advances in technology have provided customers with an abundance of choices. With so many options available, customers are harder to please than ever and less willing to accept compromises.

A second factor is an increase in the number of relevant stakeholders. Companies must answer to customers, shareholders, and employees as well as to any number of political, regulatory, and compliance authorities. Each of these groups has specific demands, and it has become penalizing for companies to satisfy one at the expense of any other.

---

requirements have become more numerous, are changing faster, and, what's more, are often in conflict with one another. We have actually measured this evolution and created what we call the BCG Complexity Index. It shows that business complexity has multiplied sixfold since 1955.[2]

Some observers think increasing business complexity is the problem. We disagree. We believe that while complexity brings immense challenges, it also offers a tremendous opportunity for companies. Increasingly, the winners in today's business environment are those companies that know how to leverage complexity and exploit it to create competitive advantage.

The real curse is not complexity so much as "complicatedness," by which we mean the proliferation of cumbersome organizational mechanisms—structures, procedures, rules, and roles—that companies put in place in an effort to deal with the mounting complexity of modern business (see the sidebar "The Complicatedness Trap"). It is this internal complicatedness, with its attendant bureaucracy, that destroys a company's ability to leverage complexity for competitive advantage. Even worse, this organizational complicatedness destroys a company's ability to get anything done. However, although complicatedness is a curse, it is not the fundamental root cause of the problem; it is, as we shall see, only a by-product of outdated, ineffectual, and irrelevant management thinking and practices.

THE COMPLICATEDNESS TRAP

Fewer Value-Adding Activities, More Useless Work on Work

The BCG Institute for Organization created an index of the number of procedures, vertical layers, interface structures, coordination bodies, scorecards, and decision approvals over the past fifteen years. Across our sample of companies, this index has increased annually by 6.7 percent, which, over the fifty-five years we studied, yields a thirty-five-fold increase.

Managers in the top quintile of the most complicated organizations spend more than 40 percent of their time writing reports and between 30 percent and 60 percent of their total work hours in coordination meetings—work on work. That doesn't leave much time for them to work with their teams, which, as a result, are often misdirected and therefore expend a lot of effort in vain. Our analysis shows that in the top quintile of complicated organizations, teams spend between 40 percent and 80 percent of their time wasting their time. It is not that teams are idle. On the contrary, they often work harder and harder but on non-value-adding activities. It means they have to do, undo, and redo, and when their efforts seem to make less and less of a difference, people lose their sense of meaning. It's hardly surprising that, based on our analysis, employees of these organizations are three times as likely to be disengaged as employees of the other companies we studied. (See figure I-1.)

FIGURE I-1

The response to complexity

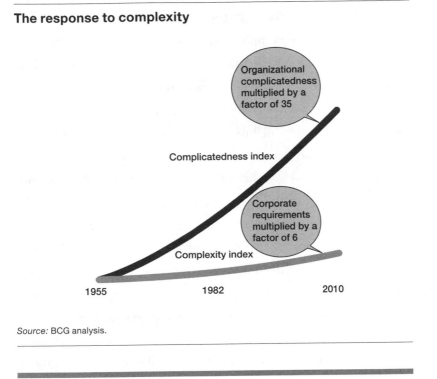

Source: BCG analysis.

But first it's necessary to understand just how pervasive and troubling the phenomenon of organizational complicatedness really is. We have done research into the rise of complicatedness, and the findings are striking. Over the past fifteen years, the number of procedures, vertical layers, interface structures, coordination bodies, scorecards, and decision approvals has increased dramatically—between 50 percent and 350 percent, depending on the company.[3]

This rapid rise in complicatedness is shocking. What also surprised us is that our analysis shows absolutely no correlation between the size of companies and their degree of complicatedness. A big company is just as likely to be relatively uncomplicated (compared to the average index) as a small company is to be very complicated. Nor is there any correlation between complicatedness and the degree of diversification. The diversity of the business portfolio does not automatically increase complicatedness. What matters, then, is not the size of the company or the number of businesses in which it competes; what matters is how the resulting business complexity is managed.[4]

Complicatedness spells trouble for a company's performance and productivity, trapping people in non-value-adding activities and causing waste and overconsumption of resources of all kinds: equipment, systems, inventories, committees, and teams. Complicatedness also has a pronounced negative effect on a company's ability to formulate a winning business strategy, causing it to miss new opportunities and fail to meet new challenges. As we have witnessed firsthand, complicatedness has deleterious effects on the human beings who are trapped in such organizations, inevitably leading to frustration, dissatisfaction, and disengagement.[5]

Indeed, we think that organizational complicatedness is the primary reason that disengagement and dissatisfaction at work have become so damaging. Surveys by The Conference Board show that the percentage of Americans who are satisfied at work declined from 61 percent in 1987 to 47 percent in 2011.[6] Studies abound on stress, burnout, work-related suicide, even death from exhaustion (the Japanese have a word for it: *karoshi*).[7]

Some argue that declining engagement is a cause of the stagnant productivity that afflicts companies, industries, and societies in many parts of the world.[8] Is it poor engagement that saps productivity?[9] Or is it the pressure to improve productivity and the discouragement people feel when efforts fail that undermine engagement at work?[10] This chicken-and-egg discussion is irrelevant; whenever we have intervened on such issues, we have always found that employee disengagement and stagnant productivity are triggered by a common factor: organizational complicatedness.

The Root Causes of Complicatedness

But, as we have hinted, complicatedness is itself only a by-product, a symptom, of the real problem. To understand the root causes of complicatedness, we must go deeper to explore a set of deeply engrained assumptions that guide how companies have responded to complexity. In struggling with the problem, most organizations have relied on two approaches with a long history in management theory and practice. We refer to them as the "hard" approach and the "soft" approach, and they are the product of two major revolutions in management theory and practice during the twentieth century and, unfortunately, remain to this day the two basic pillars of modern management. Almost all management thinking and best practice today is based on one of these two approaches, and usually a combination of the two—be it for restructuring, reorganizing, cultural transformation, reengineering, or improving engagement or motivation.

The "Hard" Approach to Management

The hard approach is the product of more than a century of managerial thinking that began with Frederick W. Taylor's work on scientific management. It was further developed in the discipline of industrial engineering and continues to this day in practices such as reengineering, restructuring, and business process design.[11]

The hard approach rests on two fundamental assumptions. The first is the belief that structures, processes, and systems have a direct and predictable effect on performance, and as long as managers pick the right ones, they will get the performance they want. So, for example, if you want your employees to customize your offering to local market demands, you choose a decentralized organizational structure; if you want to leverage economies of scale, you choose a centralized structure, and so on. The second assumption is that the human factor is the weakest and least reliable link of the organization and that it is essential to control people's behavior through the proliferation of rules to specify their actions and through financial incentives linked to carefully designed metrics and key performance indicators (KPIs) to motivate them to perform in the way the organization wants them to.

Perhaps the hard approach made sense in the past, but it is dangerously counterproductive in today's complex business environment. When the company needs to meet new performance requirements, the hard response is to add new structures, processes, and systems to help satisfy those requirements, hence, the introduction of the innovation czar, the risk management team, the compliance unit, the customer-centricity leader, Mr. Quality-in-Chief, and the cohort of coordinators and interfaces that have become so common in companies. (See the sidebar "Beyond the Org Chart.")

KEEP IN MIND

Beyond the Org Chart

Whether to organize a company by function, geography, product, customer segment, technology, or some other dimension is an issue that companies face continually. Often, an organization will cycle through various options over time.

But in an environment of complexity, whether a particular task is contained in this or that box in the org chart has become less important. Performance increasingly depends on the cooperation *between* the boxes. If you organize by function, you will have to make people cooperate to satisfy varying local customer needs. If, on the other hand, you organize by geography, you will need to make people cooperate to develop functional expertise, and so too whether you organize by product, technology, or customer segment. No matter how you arrange the boxes, there will always be performance requirements that fall between them requiring cooperation.

Even the question "Where does the P&L sit—in the regions, or the business units?" that is often at the center of discussions about organization design has little relevance any more. The proof is that companies that make the profit-and-loss statement (P&L) the cornerstone of accountability end up with multiple P&Ls—a P&L per region, per business unit, per key customer account, per product, and even sometimes per product component—in short, more complicatedness. We are not saying that organization design is unimportant. Organization design is critical. But, as we will see, it must be performed in a way very different from the current practices.

The "Soft" Approach to Management

But the hard fixes have some squeaky wheels that need greasing, and to do that companies turn to what we call the soft approach—practices such as team building, people initiatives, affiliation events, off-site retreats, and the like (all added on top of the work itself)—so that people will feel better at work and work better together. The soft approach has its main origins in the work of Elton Mayo in the 1920s, which led to the development of the human relations school of management. According to this perspective, an organization is a set of interpersonal relationships and the sentiments that govern them.[12] Good performance is the by-product of good interpersonal relationships. What people do is predetermined by personal traits, so-called psychological needs and mind-sets. In other words, to change behavior at work, change the mind-set (or change the people).

At first glance, the soft approach may seem like the antithesis to the hard approach, but it isn't. Both seek to control the individual. The only difference lies in the fact that the soft approach assumes that what really matters is emotional rather than financial stimuli. Emotional stimuli include affiliation activities, celebrations of all kinds, and the display of appropriate "leadership styles." The dynamic that these two responses to complexity produce goes something like this: the hard approach raises new obstacles for people and contributes to dissatisfaction and disengagement. Because people feel bad and ineffective, managers use the soft approach, ostensibly to help them feel and work better. Managers then assume they have addressed the problem, even though they have only addressed the symptoms. Paradoxically, this puts the onus for any continuing disengagement on the victims themselves. If problems persist (and, of course, they always do), it must be because there is something wrong with the psychology of the people involved—they have a bad attitude or the wrong mind-set. *They just don't get it.* As we shall see in some of our company examples, at its worst the soft approach can become a disguise for simple prejudice and stereotyping— for example, about the attitudes of women or young people in the workforce—leading to an enormous waste of talent and compounding ineffectiveness with injustice.

Hard and Soft Approaches Are the Root Problem

In our experience, complexity can only be addressed by people using their judgment in the moment. People's autonomy is therefore essential to deal with complexity. No amount of structure, planning, or formal rules and procedures will ever be enough to anticipate the kinds of problems people on the front line of the business will face, solutions they will need to innovate, or new opportunities they will recognize. In this respect, the human factor isn't the weak link—something to be minimized and worked around. Rather, it is the key resource for coping with complexity. Companies need to invest in—and trust—the intelligence and ingenuity of their people by expanding their autonomy and room for maneuver. Only then will employees be able to make judgments, balance complex trade-offs, find creative solutions to new problems, and do the right thing, making the best use of the available information and interpreting the rules to fulfill the spirit and not just the letter of the law. Simply piling up structure upon structure and multiplying procedures and formal rules (including some that contradict each other) with the hard approach only adds new obstacles to dealing with complexity.

It is also in the nature of complexity that no one individual has the entire answer. So it is equally necessary that people use their autonomy to cooperate with each other. Companies need to encourage—and, indeed, impel—people to perform their specialized tasks in a way that also enhances the effectiveness of others. But the more people cooperate, the harder it becomes to determine who contributed what to the ultimate solution. The proliferation of metrics and incentives of the hard approach not only adds to complicatedness but actually obstructs the kind of cooperation necessary to deal with business complexity.

These two characteristics—autonomy and cooperation—are precisely what the hard approach seeks to eliminate. Its goal is to immunize the organization against the perceived risks inherent in people's autonomy and to minimize the need for cooperation. The belief is that if the structures, processes, and systems are adequate, and that if everyone has received the necessary training and the right incentives, then everyone can remain within their silos, do what they have to do, and there will be no need for cooperation. As for the soft approach, it negates people's autonomy in using their intelligence because it views the individual's decisions and actions as Pavlovian responses to psychological needs and emotional stimuli (just as the hard approach views these decisions and actions as Pavlovian responses to financial stimuli). Moreover, as we will see in the next chapters, the emphasis on good interpersonal feelings typical of the soft approach creates obstacles to cooperation. Cooperation has nothing to do with a touchy-feely conviviality. The two pillars of current management practices are unable to handle the new challenges that corporations face. As the hard and soft approaches are being stretched beyond their limitations, companies have to resort to stitches and patches in their structure and management processes that not only fail to address complexity but also make failure increasingly costly for all stakeholders.

The Doom Loop of Management

The encounter between business complexity and the hard and soft approaches triggers a chain reaction of complicatedness and a doom loop for organizations. In front of the new complexity, the hard and soft attempts to control individuals can only create complicatedness. Complicatedness leads to stagnant productivity and disengagement, which then feed off each other. In response, companies redouble their efforts with more hard fixes and soft initiatives, which only serve to make the problem worse. (See figure I-2.)

But as we shall see, there is another way.

FIGURE I-2

The doom loop of management

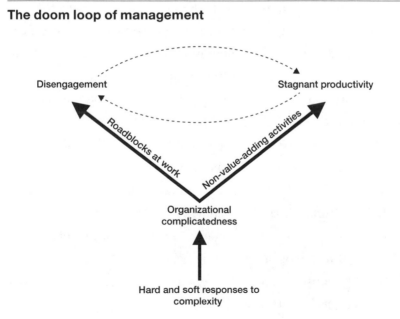

Smart Simplicity

The simple rules are a way for managers to break out of this doom loop and start moving beyond the hard and soft approaches in order to deal effectively with business complexity (see the sidebar "The Six Simple Rules Overview"). The primary goal is to create more value by better managing business complexity. However, as managers peel away the stitches and patches that have accumulated through the use of approaches that are obsolete in today's world, the by-product is also the elimination of complicatedness and its attendant costs. In this respect, the six rules constitute a third revolution in management—"smart simplicity." By helping manage complexity and remove complicatedness, the simple rules allow organizations simultaneously to improve performance and engagement. What's more, the doom loop is transformed into a virtuous circle: better performance leads to more opportunities for people; more opportunities generate more engagement; more engagement nurtures higher aspirations and contributes to even better performance.

The rules are based on the premise that the key to managing complexity is the combination of autonomy and cooperation. These are two words that people rarely think of as going together, but it is precisely the combination of the two that is required to handle complexity without complicatedness. Individual autonomy harnesses people's flexibility and agility; meanwhile, cooperation brings synergy so that everyone's efforts are multiplied in the most effective way for the group.

The purpose of the simple rules is to create situations in which each person's autonomy—in using judgment and

THE SIX SIMPLE RULES OVERVIEW

1. *Understand what your people do.* This rule is about getting a true understanding of performance—what people actually do and why they do it—and avoiding the smokescreen of the hard and soft approaches. With this understanding, you can then use the other simple rules to intervene.

2. *Reinforce integrators.* This rule involves giving to units and individuals the power and interest to foster cooperation; integrators, when reinforced, allow each one to benefit from the cooperation of others.

3. *Increase the total quantity of power.* This rule shows how to create new power—not just shift existing power—so that the organization is able to effectively mobilize people to satisfy the multiple performance requirements of complexity.

4. *Increase reciprocity.* This rule and rules five and six shift from creating the conditions for effective autonomy to ensuring that people put their autonomy in the service of the group to deal with complexity; rule four achieves this through rich objectives, the elimination of internal monopolies, and the removal of some resources.

5. *Extend the shadow of the future.* This rule harnesses the natural power of time—rather than the use of supervision, metrics, and incentives—to create direct feedback loops that impel people to do their own work today in a way that also contributes to the satisfaction of performance requirements that matter in the future.

(Continued)

6. *Reward those who cooperate.* This rule radically changes the managerial dialogue—covering the entire spectrum from target setting to evaluation—in a way that makes transparency, innovation, and ambitious aspirations become the best choice for individuals and teams.

---

energy—is made more effective by the rest of the group, and in which people put their autonomy in the service of the group. The rules are designed to create an organizational context in which cooperation becomes the best choice for each individual. In other words, these rules help organize and manage in a way that makes cooperation an individually useful behavior—a "rational strategy"—for people. The simple rules do not aim at controlling employees by imposing formal guidelines and processes; rather, they create an environment in which employees work together to develop creative solutions to complex challenges.[13] The cooperation achieved thanks to the simple rules is such that, at any time, people are mutually advantaged and impelled by others to come up with the right solutions to deal with performance requirements, even if what is right cannot be specified in advance.[14] Simplifying in a naive way—by ignoring or discarding business complexity—is a dead end. You have to be smart and play on people's smartness. You have to recognize business complexity and simplify in a way that leverages people's intelligence and judgment. The combination of autonomy and cooperation allows you to do this.

Why not fewer than six rules? We know that the six rules cannot be boiled down to fewer rules because no rule can be deducted from the five others. None of the six rules is superfluous. Vice versa, we have never encountered a situation in which the solution would not be a combination of some of the six rules. It is not necessary to add another rule. Together the six rules constitute a minimum sufficient set to confront complexity.

The first three rules are designed to give people an advantage in the way they mobilize their intelligence and energy at work by providing them with relevant knowledge, room for maneuver, power, and the resource of cooperation. The first simple rule is about understanding what people do and why they do it. The second rule is about the utilization of power to foster cooperation. The third rule is about the production of power. These first three rules create the conditions for individual autonomy so that its effectiveness can be multiplied through cooperation *from* others.

Simple rules four, five, and six are designed to impel people to confront complexity and to use their autonomy to cooperate *with* others, by embedding feedback loops that expose them as directly as possible to the consequences of their actions, without the need for extra supervision and structure or for the bureaucracy of compliance metrics and incentives. The fourth and fifth rules create direct feedback loops that are intrinsically embedded into work processes and activities. The direct feedback loops created by the fourth rule are based on interdependencies— space, so to speak. The feedback loops of the fifth rule are based on time, directly gratifying or penalizing people depending on how well they do today for tomorrow. When work processes do not allow for direct feedback loops, management intervention is needed as a last resort to close them, through evaluation. This is the role of the sixth rule.

In summary, the first three rules use the group effect to give people's autonomy an advantage in best using their energy and judgment, while the last three rules impel people to put their autonomy in the best service of the group. Whenever people apply their full energy and intelligence to the greater range of possible solutions that arises from cooperation, they are bound to reach superior solutions to those predefined or hard-wired in procedures and structures and to the loose compromises of collaboration within informal, consensus-seeking groups.

By calling the rules "simple," we don't mean to imply that they are necessarily easy to put into practice. Using them requires managers to think differently and work differently. Nor do we mean that managers should pursue simplification as a goal in itself.[15] What we do mean, however, is that these rules allow executives to create competitive advantage by exploiting complexity without getting complicated.

The Scientific Basis of the Six Simple Rules

The six rules are based on fundamental developments in the social sciences that can be traced back to the work of Herbert Simon and Thomas Schelling. Simon received the Nobel Prize in 1978 for his study of decision making, and Schelling in 2005 for his game-theoretic work on conflicts and cooperation. Simon's research brought a radically new perspective on cognitive processes, how the individual decides and acts, while Schelling's helped us better understand interactions between individuals and the effect of these interactions on overall results, which can be very different from their individual intent. Other important intellectual contributors are Michel Crozier and Robert Axelrod. Crozier started his career by studying labor movements in the United States after World War II and then created a new approach called the strategic analysis of organizations. Axelrod is a political scientist who has helped us better understand cooperation as an evolutionary process and also coined concepts we have used to name some of the simple rules.[16]

These developments have led to a variety of new perspectives on organizations and to useful insights about human behavior that are extremely relevant to how organizations manage complexity. For example:

- *Human behavior* is *strategic.* People adapt to their environment strategically (in the sense that game theory uses the term) in order to fulfill certain objectives or goals. They may be more or less conscious of those goals, but the goals can be identified by studying carefully how they act. In this respect, human behavior can always be analyzed as a rational strategy in an individual's context; there are always "good reasons" (in the sense of reasons with explanatory power) for how people behave.[17]

- *Formal rules and procedures don't have a predetermined effect on people's behavior.* Rather, people actively interpret rules and use them as a resource to fulfill their goals. What matters are not the rules, but the ways people use them.

- *Cooperation isn't just some taken-for-granted value or goal* (the desire that people "work together as a team"). It is a complex social process, hard to create and easy to destroy. Organizations have to create the right context for cooperation.

- *Power isn't a necessary evil or source of coercion.* It is a critical resource for the individual in organizations and for mobilizing collective action.

These concepts are the basis on which the six rules operate and why these rules work, especially given the complexity that is making all traditional hard and soft management approaches obsolete. Our focus with the six simple rules has been on making these concepts *actionable*—that is, to help managers to use them in their day-to-day work running business organizations. You can think of the six simple rules as guidelines for practice. Because all performance issues arise from people's actions, decisions, and interactions—what we call *behaviors* in this book—the six rules provide the basis for tackling the whole lineup of organizational challenges, including productivity, innovation, growth, and cultural transformation.

Getting Started

Each of the six chapters of this book is organized around one of the simple rules. The purpose of the simple rules is to let managers really manage, to use the tools that managers have always used—strategy setting and organizational design—but for a different end and a far more effective outcome. The rules help managers foster both autonomy and cooperation to effectively handle business complexity and prevent much organizational complicatedness. Unlike other recent books that propose new roles for managers, we focus less on psychological issues of individual motivation and one-to-one interactions and more on managing large-scale situations and the collective properties (for instance, productivity and innovation) that emerge from multiple interactions among groups, units, and teams.[18] There is a lot of loose talk these days about self-organizing systems and the end of management. Let's be clear: we believe in the essential role of management. But we contend that traditional methods, developed for a different, less complex era, are obsolete or fast becoming so. Let's begin, then, with the first fundamental rule of management, simple rule one—understand what your people do.

1

Simple Rule One

Understand What Your People Do

I n today's organizations, managers often do not know what the people who work for them actually do. Blinded by the assumptions of the hard and soft approaches, they tend to focus either on the formal descriptions of people's jobs (what they are supposed to do) or on their interpretations of people's personality and mind-set (what people are supposed to be like). As a result, managers do not properly understand people's actual behavior: what they really do.

Why does this matter? Because people's behavior at work is performance in the making. An organization's performance is nothing more than the combined effect of people's behavior— their actions, decisions, and interactions. When managers don't understand what people really do, they don't understand why the organization is performing (or not performing) the way it is. This lack of understanding helps explain why, when managers embark on performance-improvement initiatives, they often prescribe solutions that not only fail to improve performance but also add to organizational complicatedness.

In this chapter, we will show you how to do the following:

- **Analyze the work context.** People's behavior can be understood in terms of three key elements: the *goals* people are seeking to attain (or problems they are trying to solve) and the available *resources* that help them or *constraints* that hinder them. An important type of constraint is the *adjustment cost* that people bear when they cooperate with others. We call the combination of these factors the *work context*. To understand the context of people's work, you must observe them in action, study what they do, and talk with them and those around them.

- **Understand how organizational structures, processes, and systems affect the work context.** The formal structures, processes, and systems of the organization have an impact on behaviors and performance, but a very indirect one. Their impact depends on how they combine with each other to shape the goals, resources, and constraints to which people adjust their behaviors. When managers have an in-depth understanding of the dynamics shaping human behavior in the organization, they are then in a position to use the usual tools that they have available—organizational design, metrics, role definitions, and so on—to influence the work context and nudge people's behavior in a direction that will result in improved performance.[1]

- **Avoid being led astray by the hard and the soft approaches.**
  Armed with this new understanding, we will then revisit
  the hard and soft approaches to understand in more detail
  why they can only produce complicatedness. Freeing yourself from the assumptions of the hard and soft approaches
  will allow you to avoid the obfuscations that typically keep
  managers from understanding what is really going on in
  their organizations and how performance is generated
  from behavior.

Understanding what people do and why they do what they
do is so utterly fundamental that it is our simple rule one.
Before you, as a manager, do anything to solve a performance
problem, you can save yourself a lot of time and money by first
applying this rule. To illustrate the value of the first simple
rule, we will tell the story of what we call InterLodge, a travel
and tourism company we worked with to improve the performance of its hotel unit, interspersing the story with segments of analysis and interpretation. (Like all the companies
described in the book, this is a real company, but we have
changed the name.) The management of InterLodge made
two attempts to improve performance based on the hard
and soft approaches. Neither succeeded because both fundamentally misunderstood the problem. Finally, the organization came fully to understand the behaviors that were
causing the poor performance in the hotels. InterLodge was
then able to make relatively modest changes that, by shifting the context, resulted in new behaviors that generated
performance improvements well beyond management's initial
expectations.

InterLodge: A Bold Commitment to Improve

The management team at InterLodge faced a big problem: the company's share price was declining and had been falling for some time. Costs were too high and profitability was too low. Both the occupancy rate and the average price point per room were below target. According to surveys the company had conducted, customer satisfaction was far from what it should be.

The solution to these problems, the management team decided, was to embark on a set of restructuring and reengineering initiatives. It created a shared services program to serve groups of hotels by region, which it believed would reduce costs and also result in a higher and more consistent quality in the hotels' services, amenities, and fixtures. It recast or redefined some roles and responsibilities of hotel employees with the goal of improving productivity and also focusing resources more sharply on quality. Finally, it rolled out a new, computerized, yield management system that it hoped would improve occupancy rate.

A year later, none of these changes had produced any of the improvements the management team sought. The occupancy rate and average room price had not gone up. Customer satisfaction scores had not improved. Profitability remained below target. The share price continued to slide.

Concerned (and a little bit panicked), the management team decided to take a bold step: in a public announcement, InterLodge committed to doubling its share price within three years. The intent of this commitment was to boost shareholder confidence and, just as important, energize the organization's own people. The commitment had a powerful effect on Inter-Lodge employees, particularly the hotel managers, but it was the opposite of what management had intended. They were not so much energized as terrified. The hotels were expected to increase the occupancy rate, boost the average price point, and improve customer satisfaction all at the same time. How could they possibly do that? They had no choice but to work with the shared services offerings and the centralized yield management systems, so there was little they could do with those aspects of their operations. The organization—including reporting structure, roles and responsibilities, and staffing levels—had been carefully designed in the restructuring initiative and could not be altered yet again.

So, the hotel managers looked for other ways to make improvements and settled on customer satisfaction as the element they could most influence. They came to the conclusion that an important cause of dissatisfaction was the interactions that guests had with hotel staff. They felt that the hotel receptionists, in particular, were a problem. These junior staff had the most contact with guests, but their customer engagement skills were limited to handling basic transactions. The managers also felt there was an issue with the type of person who typically held this (relatively low-paid) position. They were generally young and just didn't seem to care that much about doing a good job. They certainly had no loyalty to the job or to the company, as evidenced by the high turnover rate in the position. The sales people who were primarily responsible for increasing the occupancy rate agreed. The receptionists, they said, often did not sell rooms to travelers who arrived late in the day even when rooms were available; instead they simply said that the hotel was full. This approach made absolutely no economic sense.

The management team at InterLodge took three actions to address the problems with the receptionists. First, executives further clarified the roles, scorecards, and process definitions for reception. Second, they put the receptionists through a training program to improve their skills in "guest engagement," on the theory that better interactions would make guests happier. Third, they set up an incentive plan to motivate receptionists to sell more rooms and help increase the occupancy rate.

Six months later, however, the problems remained. In fact, things had gotten worse. The occupancy rate had dropped further. Average price point was down. Customer surveys showed *lower* levels of satisfaction. Receptionist turnover had risen.

Needless to say, by this point, the management team at Inter-Lodge was extremely frustrated. The company had invested considerable resources in the two rounds of improvement initiatives—first, the restructuring and reengineering, and then the incentivizing and training. What else could it do?

The answer: it could do the most important thing of all—understand what its people were actually doing and why, starting with the context of the work in the hotels.

Analyze the Work Context

To understand what people do and why they do it, you need to understand the context of their work. This context is composed of three elements: goals, resources, and constraints.[2] Behaviors are the solutions people find to deal with their problems and achieve their goals, given the resources and constraints they encounter in their situation at work. In this sense, behaviors must be treated as *rational strategies*. People may not always be right in what they choose to do. They make mistakes. Still, their behavior is always a solution they have found to deal with what matters to them. If they had found a better solution, they would do something else. What's more, all the organizational mechanisms—structures, procedures, scorecards, incentives, and so on—that managers typically think drive performance are really only resources or constraints that employees will use or try to sidestep to achieve their goals. These organizational mechanisms certainly influence behavior, and thus performance, but only indirectly and often in a counterintuitive way. It all depends on how people use them.

Form Hypotheses about Goals, Resources, and Constraints

To determine the context, you have to gather information and data about the work, develop a hypothesis about why people behave as they do, and then test your hypothesis with further observation and data gathering. Once you understand what people do and why they do it, it is easier to improve performance, not by asking or telling people what to do, but by changing their context. You'll end up using fewer and more-appropriate organizational mechanisms, creating more value at lower costs.

Goals. Goals are what people are trying to achieve, the problems they are trying to solve, and the stakes for them in a particular situation. When you observe behaviors and learn

SIMPLE RULES TOOLKIT

Questions to Ask to Analyze Context

What are the most interesting aspects of your work? Why?

What are the most difficult, annoying, or frustrating aspects? Why?

What are the key problems that you have to deal with in your job?

- How do you go about solving them?

- How can you know if these solutions work?

Who (departments, people) do you have to interact with to do your job?

- Which interactions are the most important ones for your work? Why?

- Which are the most difficult or involve the most conflict? Why?

Who do you depend on?

- What is it that they do that affects your ability to do well?

- When they act, do they take into account the impact of their actions on you?

The answers to these questions provide the raw materials to start the analysis of the context.

Adapted with permission from Erhard Friedberg, "L'Analyse sociologique des organizations," *Pour*, special issue (Paris: L'Harmattan, 1987).

about what people do through conversations or interviews, ask yourself: to what kind of problem is this behavior a solution? What goal does it help people achieve? (See the sidebar "Questions to Ask to Analyze Context.")

As you try to answer these questions, do not think only about the formal goals set by the performance management system or by job definitions. It's not the formal goals of the organization that you want to understand, but rather the actual goals of individuals and work groups that, in fact, may not have much to do with the organization's formal goals. Instead, try to determine the problems people are trying to solve in their day-to-day activities and what is at stake for them personally in a particular situation.

The real goals and problems people are dealing with are not so easy to determine. This is partly because individuals are usually unable to articulate their goals, even when you ask them directly. Or they may know their real goals but will not tell you for any number of reasons. For instance, they may fear that you will use this information against them. For this reason, what people say in interviews and conversations must always be considered along with other sources of information such as direct observation of actions and interactions. You can then triangulate this data to figure out what is really going on.

Resources. Resources are what people use to solve their problems in achieving what matters to them at work. Some typical resources include an individual's skills and unique strengths, the cooperation of colleagues, time, information, budget, and power (for example, being able to influence something that matters to other people). What some people perceive as a resource, others can perceive as a constraint.

Constraints. Constraints are things that people try to avoid, minimize, or sidestep. Constraints hinder or restrict them in achieving the goals that matter to them. A person's constraints may include things such as performance targets, specific organizational rules, lack of room for maneuver, or dependency on others to achieve what he or she wants to achieve. Constraints are inherent to organizations. Like resources, they are neither good nor bad in themselves; these are analytical concepts to understand why people do what they do.

Assess the Adjustment Costs

A particular type of constraint is especially important in organizations. It concerns how behaviors combine with each other in producing overall results. As you analyze the work context, you will notice interdependencies among people. Whenever the work one person does has an impact on the ability of other people to do what they have to do, there are interdependencies. Whenever there is interdependency, there needs to be cooperation. To cooperate is to take into account in what you do—in your decisions and your actions—the needs and situations of others. It may mean providing them with more resources—information, knowledge, equipment, or time. It may also mean removing some of their constraints. As a result, cooperation gives others a broader range of possible solutions. It increases their ability to deal with their own tasks which enhances their effectiveness.

But cooperation is anything but easy, and you should not assume that it is happening in your organization. Cooperation between individuals with distinct responsibilities, resources, and constraints always involves what we call adjustment costs. Imagine a continuum of cooperation as a line between two end points. One of them represents what is ideal for one person in the situation; the other marks the ideal for the other person. When two

FIGURE 1-1

The cooperation continuum

A, B: an actor, i.e., a function, unit, team, or individual with specific goals, resources, and constraints.

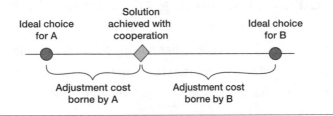

people cooperate, they move the cursor along the continuum to a spot that is not ideal for either but that is more beneficial for the overall results. The distance between each one's ideal and the solution they reach when cooperating is the cost of adjustment borne by each. Although the overall result is greater for the group as a whole, the adjustment comes at a personal cost for each individual. This cost can be professional, emotional, reputational, or, of course, financial. The adjustment cost for individuals is by no means lessened by the possibility of sharing the benefits that accrue from cooperation. (See figure 1-1.)

Adjustment costs are signals at the level of the individual for how behaviors combine with each other to produce a given performance. When people use their autonomy to avoid cooperation, then someone else has to adjust. Often, it is other people in the organization. But sometimes, it is people external to the organization—for example, customers who bear the consequences in terms of defects, delays, or higher prices, or shareholders who get lower returns because of the dysfunctions in the organization. That's why it is critical for management to understand the dynamics of adjustment costs and how they affect organizational performance. (See the sidebar "Clues for Assessing Adjustment Costs.")

SIMPLE RULES TOOLKIT

Clues for Assessing Adjustment Costs

- *Stress or dissatisfaction.* When one person or group adjusts to the needs of others, but the others do not do so in return, the result is usually a situation of high stress for those bearing the costs of adjustment.

- *Resentment.* When a person or group avoids adjusting to the needs of others, and forces them to do the adjusting, that person or group is often the target of resentment.

- *Indifference.* When a person or group neither makes adjustments nor forces others to do so, others often display indifference toward the individual or group.

Look for Anomalies

When you have identified the goals, resources, and constraints for a specific set of people or work groups, you often come up against anomalies—something that doesn't quite fit with the behaviors you observe. For example, you might discover that something you consider to be a resource is not being used by people; managers don't use the new IT system or the evaluation forms provided by the human resources department. Alternatively, you might find people spending a lot of time preoccupied with issues that to you look like they should be constraints—for instance, managers complaining bitterly about administrative tasks, but then spending hours in their office working on them.

Such anomalies are always a good sign: you start to really understand performance and how it is generated precisely when you discover things that people do that you did not expect. When that happens, you must dig into the anomaly instead of disregarding it. Indeed, if you are not finding anything unexpected or unusual, that is probably a sign that you are missing key aspects of the work context and are still too focused on org charts, process descriptions, models, or ready-made assumptions.

The point is, nothing is inherently a resource or constraint; it depends on people's goals and problems. To return to a previous example, the administrative burden that managers complain about might actually be a resource if their real goal is to avoid interacting with teams over which they have no real power. Although they may complain about it, such work provides a way to stay in the office and avoid confronting their lack of power. Dynamics such as this are why observing behaviors is so important. A resource is what people use. If people don't use something, then it's not a resource but, rather, it must be a constraint for them.

Looking for anomalies is important because resources and constraints aren't immutable. They are reversible, depending on situations. When the goal or problem changes, a resource can become a constraint and vice versa. What's more, goals, resources, and constraints are always in dynamic interaction: each partly determines the other. People do not necessarily set a goal and then look for the resources to achieve it. People adjust their goals to the available resources as much as they try to adjust resources to meet a goal. People often set ambitions and discover new aspirations according to the opportunities their resources make it possible to pursue.[3]

It's like when you play poker with your friends. Is your goal to win? Often, it depends on the cards you have been dealt. If the cards are poor, you will probably lose interest in the game. Your attention will focus somewhere else: you might check out the TV that is on in the background, start a conversation with one of the other players, pour yourself a drink. Your goal is not to win the game but simply to have a good time. But when you are dealt good cards in the next round, suddenly winning the game seems possible. You pay closer attention. You reengage. Your goal is to win.

As in a poker game, so too in organizations. Often, the most effective way to change people's goals is not to intervene directly on the goals, but rather to change the resources available to the people. They will then adjust their goals to the new resources and reengage.

Analyzing the Work Context at InterLodge

Now let us try to understand the work context of the receptionists at InterLodge. We got involved with the organization after the failure of the two previous attempts to improve performance. Together with an internal team of salespeople, we spent a month observing and talking with receptionists in several hotels in order to understand the problems they were trying to solve, the goals they were trying to achieve, and their resources and constraints.

The team discovered that by far the most difficult part of the job for the receptionists was dealing with customer complaints. These complaints were usually about maintenance issues such as a broken TV, a faulty bathroom faucet, or a malfunctioning heater. Part of the problem was that although the hotel's housekeepers were in the rooms to clean them every day, they were so focused on hitting their productivity targets that they either didn't notice the problem or didn't report it to maintenance when they did (because it required so much interaction and time that their productivity would diminish). They just kept on cleaning the rooms as if everything were OK. The receptionists had to bear the consequences of this insufficient cooperation between housekeeping and maintenance.

Typically, what would happen is that the guest would discover the problem when he or she checked in (or returned to the room) in the evening, then call reception to complain. But by then, the maintenance office was closed for the day, and it would simply take too long to locate someone to perform an emergency repair. The receptionists had to deal with the angry customers on their own.

Receptionists spend their work lives dealing with customers. When angry customers shout at them, their lives at work become hell. By talking to the receptionists, the team developed an insight that may seem obvious in retrospect, but actually took a lot of work to develop: the goal of the receptionist was not so much to earn a financial incentive by improving the occupancy rate. No, the goal of receptionists was to avoid the unpleasantness of dealing with unhappy customers.

The constraint of the receptionists was that they were dependent on the functions of housekeeping and maintenance. These two functions determined whether the receptionists' work was hell or not. How did the receptionists behave in this context? They turned to three solutions that allowed them to exploit the resources available to them:

- *Personal attention.* When customers complained, receptionists—especially the younger and more energetic ones—would start by trying to fix the problem themselves, running back and forth between the front desk and the problem rooms. But this behavior only annoyed the other customers who had showed up at the reception desk for check-in in the meantime and had to wait for the receptionist to return. So, in addition to having to compensate for the deficiencies of housekeeping and maintenance, they were also blamed by customers and management for providing poor service. This double bind was a major factor in their high turnover rate.

- *Keeping rooms in reserve.* One way receptionists could calm angry customers was to offer them a new room. Even if the new room wasn't so much better, upset customers tended to appreciate a receptionist who went out of his or her way to help in this fashion. That was a pretty good solution for the receptionist but not so good for the organization. It was precisely this behavior that was contributing to the low occupancy rate, because the receptionists would hold empty rooms in reserve in anticipation of needing them to mollify unhappy customers.

- *Adjusting the price.* Sometimes, receptionists would also apply their newfound customer-engagement skills to negotiate a refund, rebate, or voucher with an angry customer. This diffused customer anger, but it didn't improve the guest experience, and it lowered the hotel's average price point.

(For an illustration of this analysis, see figure 1-2.)

As you can see from this analysis, the young receptionists were forced to bear the adjustment costs caused by the behavior of the back-office functions. They had little choice in the matter; somehow, they had to deal with the angry customers. The adjustment costs they suffered were simultaneously financial (they didn't

FIGURE 1-2

The receptionists' context

Actors	Goals/ problems	Resources	Constraints	Behaviors	
Hotel receptionists	Avoid problems with customers	Empty rooms	Most exposed to customers	Personal attention to compensate for back offices	Poor customer experience

High staff turnover |
| | | New customer-facing skills | Dependent on back offices and bearing the conse-quences of their insuf-ficient coop-eration | Keeping rooms in reserve | Under-utilization of capacity |
| | | | | Adjusting the price | Declining price point |

41

achieve their bonus), emotional (they were blamed by both managers and customers), and professional (at a certain point, they would become so burned out that they would quit, sacrificing their tenure at the company in order to start from scratch somewhere else).

But customers were also bearing adjustment costs in the form of a poor hotel experience. And, of course, so were the company's shareholders in the form of declining returns, caused by the underutilization of hotel capacity, the lower price point, and increased costs (notably, the cost of recruiting new receptionists). When people avoid cooperation and externalize the adjustment costs to third parties, it is always at the expense of the organization. Receptionists could never fully compensate for what the back-office functions could have achieved had they been cooperating with each other.

As a result of this analysis, InterLodge management finally had an accurate understanding of the (rational, given the context) behaviors that generated the poor performance at the company's hotels. But before telling you what we and senior managers at the company did to fix the problem, let's revisit precisely why it took them so long to understand what was really going on.

How the Hard Approach Gets in the Way of Understanding Performance

According to the hard approach, performance is a direct consequence of what an organization's members are instructed and given incentives to do. This assumption explains why the hard approach insists so much on clarity—in the details, completeness, and accuracy of job and role definitions, process instructions, procedural rules, and so on. Structure defines the role, processes instruct how to perform it, and incentives motivate the right person in the right role to do it. From this perspective, if there is a performance problem, then it must be because some key organizational element is missing or not detailed enough. So companies jump straight from identifying a performance problem to deploying new structures, processes, or systems to resolve it. This error dumps a first layer of complicatedness into the organization.

This is precisely what happened at InterLodge. The management team restructured and reengineered without really understanding what people did and why they did it. Only after a full year of disappointing results did it start to pay attention to the front-line. What did it conclude? Receptionists were not selling rooms to latecomers. They were not engaging the customers in a way that made customers satisfied. They were not charging the right room rate. But this is not what the receptionists were doing; it is what they were *not* doing.

Too often, diagnostics focus on what people fail to do. *Our sales team does not do cross-selling. Our managers are not making decisions. Our engineers are not innovating.* Yet, people do not spend their days not cross-selling, not deciding, not innovating. They do things—what and why? We do not focus on what people do, but on what they don't do. Therefore we cannot understand *why* they do what they do. So, how can we change it? The hard approach dictates that we just add new incentives, new processes, new structures. In doing so, we complicate matters without tackling the root causes.

When you think about it, to focus on what people fail to do as opposed to what they do is a fundamentally backward way of addressing a performance problem. But given the assumptions embedded in the hard approach, it is really not so surprising. Since what matters in the hard approach are the procedural instructions, then problems must be caused by people who deviate from the formal procedures, in other words, by a *gap* in what they do. When managers identify such a gap, they assume that it must be due to an equivalent gap in the formal procedures, perhaps a lack of clarity in the instructions or some missing organizational structure or system that needs to be added. At InterLodge for instance, the lack of selling was explained by a lack of incentives to sell.

Diagnoses based on the hard approach are full of similar explanations, what you might call the "root-cause by absence": "We are not innovative enough because we have no innovation strategy." Or: "Our trains are late because we have no punctuality function." Then, the next step is to add a new organizational element to bridge the gap: a team to develop an innovation strategy (with a whole new set of dedicated processes and performance requirements) or a scheduling and punctuality group to make sure the trains run on time. That's why the hard approach generates complicatedness.

To be clear, we are not saying that organizational elements like structures, processes, and systems are somehow unimportant. Performance is what it is, because people do what they do, not because of what they don't do. People do what they do precisely because of the organizational elements already in place (not because of the ones that are missing). In contrast to the assumptions of the hard approach, however, these elements do not have a direct and easy-to-anticipate effect on either behavior or performance. The effect they have depends on how they combine to shape the context of goals, resources, and constraints to which people adjust their actions. The issue is not that organizational elements need to be consistent with one another. *With this type of structure you need that kind of process.* Judgments like these are most often meaningless. Organizational elements do not combine with each other in the abstract, based on their supposed and intrinsic pros and cons. It is impossible to know how they combine by just considering their characteristics. It is only by considering the work context, and their effect in this context, that organizational elements can be appropriately analyzed and designed. The effect of organizational elements on behaviors, thus performance, depends on how people deal with these elements as resources or constraints.

Think back to the situation of the hotel receptionists. The new skills they acquired through the training programs became a resource to cope with their real goal, which was to avoid stressful encounters with angry customers. So they used their skills not to meet the target price point but to proactively offer rebates and refunds. What's more, their new skills combined with their clarified roles in an unexpected way that also provided new resources to the receptionists, but not in the way that management intended: some receptionists used their newfound interaction skills to explain clearly to guests that their responsibilities stopped at the front desk and did not include back-office activities (which, of course, only angered the customers still further and led to more rebates).

What about the financial incentives to maintain high-capacity utilization? They had little effect on sales because the receptionists' behavior was not "not to sell rooms to latecomers" but rather to keep rooms in reserve. They were not passively omitting to sell because of a lack of incentives; they were making a choice that provided them with the resource of unoccupied rooms. The incentive scheme—which showed receptionists how much they *could* have earned—only increased their frustration and turnover.

The actual impact of the training and incentive scheme at Inter-Lodge shows that when it comes to complicatedness, if an organizational mechanism is useless, then it is positively damaging. We sometimes hear managers say, "Well, it may not help much but at least it won't do any harm." This is a mistaken belief. All organizational initiatives always have some effect—even if indirect—on the work context, so useless initiatives or mechanisms are actually counterproductive; they do damage. To add something useless is at least as dangerous as removing something that is necessary.

When companies select organizational elements according to their supposed effects on performance requirements, without paying attention to people's rationality in between, it is a bit like spinning an organizational roulette wheel. The more requirements there are, the more costly the roulette becomes for employees, customers, and shareholders.

How the Soft Approach Gets in the Way of Understanding Performance

In contrast to the hard approach, the soft approach views performance as a by-product of good interpersonal relationships. But this view confuses people getting along with genuinely productive cooperation. Real cooperation is not all fun and games. As we said earlier, it always involves adjustment costs. To be sure, when people hate each other, they tend not to cooperate. But, beyond a certain threshold, good feelings don't help either.

Indeed, the better the feelings among individuals in a group, the more people are likely to avoid straining the relationship by bearing adjustment costs themselves or by imposing them on others within the group. So, they will avoid cooperation and make third parties bear the consequences, or they will compensate with extra resources that remove interdependencies. (Think how convenient it is to have multiple TVs at home: that way, family members don't have to do the hard work of cooperating over what show to watch at a given time.) In the workplace, the extra resources take the form, not of TVs, but of excess inventory stocks, time delays, interfaces and committees, and customer requirements unmet.

The other feature of the soft approach is that behaviors are assumed to be driven by people's personal traits and mind-sets. This belief is inspired by an overreliance on psychology typical of the soft approach. "To change behaviors, you must first change the mind-set" is the mantra. When this doesn't work, diagnoses based on the soft approach end up putting the blame on people's personality and values. At InterLodge for example, both management and some work groups (like the sales teams) initially assumed that receptionists were somehow inherently disengaged and irresponsible because of their relative youth. We've seen similar kinds of stereotyping at other companies. But the high turnover rate at InterLodge was not caused by psychological factors or stereotypical behaviors, such as a supposed lack of loyalty on the part of the younger generation. On the contrary, the oldest and longest-serving receptionists were the ones who cared the *least* about the hotel and customer satisfaction. They had started their careers when customer satisfaction was less of a concern (because there was less competitive pressure). As the competitive pressure increased, these longer-serving receptionists had been able to learn the tricks (resources) to protect themselves from customer pressure.

Much like the hard approach, the soft approach has it backwards. To change behavior, it is more effective to change the context instead of trying to change people's mind-sets. When the context changes, behaviors adjust, and when people behave the way they do, their values, feelings, and mentalities evolve accordingly. These psychological factors do not drive change; they are consequences. Think about the implications for cooperation. We often hear that to get people to cooperate, we first need to instill trust. This never works because change goes the other way round. When the goals, resources, and constraints are changed for some people, cooperation may become an individually useful behavior for them. As they start to cooperate, with more or less success depending on how the context of others has also changed, trust in these others will eventually evolve, creating a self-reinforcing loop when outcomes match expectations. By the way, even modern psychology has come to recognize the decisive importance of the context. As Eldar Shafir, professor of psychology and public policy at Princeton University, has recently put it, "Human behavior tends to be heavily context dependent. One of the major lessons of modern psychological research is the impressive power that the situation exerts, along with a persistent tendency on our part to underestimate this power relative to the presumed influence of personal intentions and traits."[4] The decisive role of the context does not contradict the notion of autonomy. Far from it. Taking into account people's autonomy matters precisely because behaviors are intelligent—strategic and adaptive—ways to adjust to a context, rather than the automatic and passive implementation of supposedly predefined responses.

Of course, sometimes managers do pay attention to people's behavior. We hear executives say, "We've created a new organizational structure, but in order for it to deliver, people need to behave differently." Perspectives like this are probably the most pernicious of all. The hard approach defines the new organizational structure, and the soft approach defines the behavior necessary to function effectively within that structure. But behaviors do not come on top of or in addition to organizational elements. They are consequences—even if indirect and often surprising—of these elements. If the context is in contradiction with the behaviors advertised on corporate posters, people become distrustful, even cynical, of the planned changes.

The Result at InterLodge

So what happened at InterLodge? Once the management team took the time to understand the context of the work in its hotels, it came to realize that the problem was not that the receptionists were badly trained, or had some psychological issue or attitude problem, or needed more incentives. Rather, their behaviors were rational solutions to the problems they faced. (See the sidebar "Behaviors Are Rational Solutions in a Particular Context.")

The management team took three steps to create a new work context both for the receptionists and for the back-office housekeeping and maintenance functions. (Here, we will focus on the high level of *what* the senior executives did. In the next chapter, we will get into more detail about precisely *how* it did it because the *how* depended on the use of simple rule two.)

KEEP IN MIND

Behaviors Are Rational Solutions in a Particular Context

- People always have reasons for the things they do, even if those things are not always reasonable from the perspective of others.

- Every behavior is a solution to a problem.

- Every behavior contains evidence about the resources it mobilizes.

- Every behavior shows traces of the efforts people make to side-step or minimize their constraints.

- Never explain what people do in terms of an irrational mind-set (doing so tells more about the limitations of your analysis than the limitations of the people being analyzed).

- *Removed useless and thus counterproductive organizational elements.* First, the company got rid of the hard and soft initiatives that weren't really addressing the problem. They ended the receptionist "guest engagement" training program and eliminated the financial incentives that were supposed to improve room occupancy but had failed to do so.

- *Adjusted career paths.* Traditionally, managers at InterLodge advanced in the organization by rising within their specific function. Another change that senior management made was to make managerial promotion dependent on having worked in more than one function. The purpose of this change was to ensure that all managers got a firsthand understanding of what people actually did in multiple functions and how the work in each function related to the work in other functions.

- *Changed the context to produce cooperation.* The management team gave the receptionists some power over housekeeping and maintenance. The purpose of this change was to impel those functions to cooperate with each other and with the front-office staff in solving customer problems, so the receptionists would not have to rely on rebates or spare rooms (thus creating a context in which those were no longer a *resource*). We will say a lot more about this change in the next chapter.

These relatively minor changes had a dramatic impact on performance. Instead of doubling its share price in three years, InterLodge nearly tripled its share price in two years.

This first simple rule—understanding what your people do and how it generates performance—is an essential precursor to any organizational change. Instead of jumping directly from performance issues to the creation of new structures, processes, and systems, you must seek to understand the root causes of performance at the level of the behaviors and the factors that shape those behaviors. This accuracy of understanding creates conditions such that fewer and more effective structures, processes, and systems can be established in the organization design. (See the sidebar "Performance Is Behavior.")

KEEP IN MIND

Performance Is Behavior

Performance is the result of what people do—their actions, interactions, and decisions.

To understand organizational performance, managers must trace that performance back to what people do and the way their behaviors combine with each other to produce overall results.

- Describe what people do, not what they don't do.

- Identify their goals, resources, and constraints.

- Understand how existing organizational elements shape these goals, resources, and constraints.

- Don't use black-box explanations based on people's mind-sets or personality traits.

- Ask yourself how behaviors adjust to each other and how those adjustments shape performance.

When you know what people do and why they do it—without referring to generic pros and cons that are supposed to characterize structures, processes, and systems, or to missing organizational elements, or to pseudo-psychology, stereotyping, or *ad hominem* explanations—you can take steps to change the context of what people do, increase cooperation, and improve overall performance. The remaining simple rules give you ways to do just that.

SUMMARY OF SIMPLE RULE ONE

What do the executive teams of competing firms actually compete on? Not on their firm's products or services—this is the company's output. On the pertinence of their decisions? This is quite tautological. In fact, executive teams primarily compete on the quality of their insights about their own organization. The first basis of competition between executive teams is the understanding of what really happens in their organization. To deal with complexity without complicatedness requires that you must first avoid or get rid of the false explanations derived from the hard and soft approaches that obscure your understanding of what is really going on. You need to get a true understanding of performance: what people do and why they do it.

- Trace performance back to behaviors and how they influence and combine with each other to produce overall results. Use observation, mapping, measurement, and discussion to do this.

- Understand the context of goals, resources, and constraints within which the current behaviors constitute *rational strategies* for people.

- Find out how your organization's elements (structure, scorecards, systems, incentives, and so on) shape these goals, resources, and constraints.

- Because you understand why people do what they do and how it drives performance, you have created the *sine qua non* conditions to then define with surgical accuracy the minimum sufficient set of interventions. You are now ready to use the other simple rules to modify and simplify the organizational elements with adequate knowledge of their impact on the work context and thus performance.

2

Simple Rule Two

Reinforce Integrators

A n integrator is an individual or a work unit that fosters cooperation for the company's benefit. Given that cooperation is central to addressing business complexity, integrators play a critical role in the organization. That's why "reinforcing integrators" is our second simple rule.

In this chapter, you will learn:

- **How integrators are different from traditional coordinators.** An effective integrator has both an interest in making others cooperate and the power to impel them to do so. Integrators ensure that the organization can satisfy multiple performance requirements without layers of structure and rules. They can replace complicated matrix structures. An integrator is the opposite of a coordinator, a dedicated overlay, or a middle office.

- **How to identify potential integrators in the organization.** Anybody can play the integrator role as part of his or her existing job. But some individuals or work groups are better placed to be effective integrators than others. Some already have an interest in fostering cooperation; others have the power (but not yet the interest) to do so. Reinforcing integrators involves making sure that there are roles in the organization with both the power and the interest.

- **Transform managers into integrators.** You don't need to be a manager to play the role of integrator. But when you think about it, being an integrator should be at the very heart of the managerial role. Yet, because of their reliance on the hard and soft approaches, few managers today function effectively as integrators. We will show the steps that senior executives can take to address this problem, allowing them to transform their managers into integrators whose primary mission is to generate constructive cooperation throughout the organization.

To illustrate the importance of the integrator role, in this chapter we will tell the story of a company we call MobiliTele, a manufacturer of the technological infrastructure for cellular telephone networks. MobiliTele's product development process was consistently and egregiously late in delivering new products. When hard fixes didn't work, MobiliTele used the first two simple rules to speed significantly the development of its products.

How Integrators Are Different

Organizations are literally swamped with dedicated roles designed to help different parts work better with each other: coordinators, cross-functional committees, interface groups, overlays, and the like. These roles and functions are the exact opposite of what we mean by integrators because, first, they are not very effective and, second, they contribute to organizational complicatedness.

There are three things that distinguish integrators from these traditional hard solutions. First, being an integrator is not a dedicated job. Rather, it is a role in the organizational system that an individual plays as part of his or her usual job. It is not a matter of function, but of functioning—a way to perform one's function. In other words, you can reinforce integrators without adding to complicatedness.

Second, unlike people in coordination roles, integrators do not intervene after the fact, reviewing the compatibility of the separate inputs provided by various units and then starting an iterative sequence of modifications. Rather, integrators are directly involved in the cooperation, where the action takes place and where the richest sources of information are. By helping units benefit from the cooperation of others, they are a resource to these units. But they also function as a healthy constraint, compelling units to bear the adjustment costs inherent to cooperation when it is for the greater good of the organization.

Third, unlike traditional coordinator roles that people working in the critical path of the business can easily ignore, integrators cannot be ignored. As a result, they are often the focus of very strong emotions. Because they are a resource and a constraint, integrators typically attract positive and negative feelings, but never indifference. You can use this fact as a clue when identifying potential candidates for the integrator role in your organization. (See the sidebar "Identifying Potential Integrators.")

SIMPLE RULES TOOLKIT

Identifying Potential Integrators

The feelings people express about their work or the work of others can provide initial clues to identify those individuals or work groups that are good candidates to play the integrator role. For example:

- *Those who express high levels of dissatisfaction at work.*
  These people are usually at a nexus where constraints and requirements meet. Their dissatisfaction is usually the result of having to bear most of the adjustment costs because others are not cooperating with them. They have an interest in improving cooperation but not yet the power to do so.

- *Those who are resented by others.* Being the focus of resentment is often a sign that individuals or work groups have the power to make others bear the adjustment costs of cooperation instead of themselves. Paradoxically, this is a signal that they have their hands on the levers of cooperation and are using this power to their own advantage. Shifting the work context to provide such people with an interest to cooperate with others can turn them into effective integrators for the benefit of the organization as a whole.

Creating Integrators in Existing Work Roles

When you look across your company, no matter how it may be organized—back offices, front offices, R&D, manufacturing, sales, product groups, business units, and the like—you can find potential integrators. One obvious place to look is among those individuals or groups in the organization who have an interest in cooperation but not the power to impel others to cooperate with them. These are people who, because they lack power, are forced to bear the bulk of the adjustment costs because others do not cooperate with them.

You've already met one such group: the receptionists at InterLodge. Their work put them in the closest contact with customers, and they were the most directly penalized when customers were unhappy. They had an interest in cooperation but had no way to influence the behavior of other groups—specifically, the housekeeping and maintenance staffs.

There was no practical way to directly expose the housekeepers and maintenance workers to the wrath of the unhappy customer. But the receptionists could be given a say in the evaluation and promotion of these coworkers. So, one of the specific changes that management at InterLodge made was to give the receptionists a say in the performance evaluation of the housekeeping and maintenance personnel. In the past, it had always been enough for these employees to fulfill the criteria and meet the targets of their individual function. Now, people in the two back-office functions were also being evaluated on how effectively they cooperated with each other and with the receptionists, and it was the opinion of the receptionists themselves that carried a special weight.

With this simple change, the opinions and context of receptionists suddenly mattered a great deal to the housekeepers and the people in maintenance in a way that it had never mattered before. They now had a clear interest to cooperate with each other and with the receptionists. After all, their careers and the possibility of promotion were on the line. When this change in how personnel in the back-office functions were evaluated was combined with the new cross-functional rotation of managers (which gave managers more of an appreciation for the interdependencies among the various functions), the nature of work changed rapidly at the hotel. The housekeepers checked the equipment in the rooms when they cleaned and let the maintenance group know immediately when something needed attention. What's more, the two back-office functions were a lot more responsive when someone from reception would call asking for help to resolve a customer problem.

This increased cooperation enabled the company to better meet its multiple performance requirements:

- *Customer satisfaction.* Because the rooms were clean and the equipment worked, customer satisfaction started to rise.

- *Average room rate.* Because the guests were happier with their rooms, the receptionists had to rely less and less on giving them rebates, so average room rate improved.

- *Higher occupancy rate.* Because the receptionists no longer felt they had to hold rooms in reserve—just in case a problem did arise—they sold more rooms, and occupancy rates rose.

- *Lower turnover rate.* Once the receptionists were more satisfied at work, the turnover rate in the position was reduced by a factor of six, which cut recruiting cost.

- *Greater economies of scale.* The cooperation of housekeeping and maintenance resulted in more preventive maintenance, solving problems before they had a chance to occur and affect customers; the company was thus able to further regroup the maintenance function at the regional level.

- *Elimination of complicatedness.* The useless and counterproductive training efforts, the elaborate role definitions and performance scorecards, and related controls and incentives were all eliminated.

Thanks to these improvements, InterLodge hotel business unit's gross margin increased by 20 percent within eighteen months. The rapid improvement in margins allowed the company to surpass its already ambitious goal of doubling its stock price in three years and to nearly triple it in just two years.

By reinforcing the receptionists as integrators, InterLodge was able to create a genuinely customer-centric organization. As before, the receptionists were at the center of the customers' interactions at the hotel; they were the employees that customers met and talked to when something went wrong. But now, the receptionists had the power to actually do something about it, by making the housekeepers and maintenance staff cooperate in solving and avoiding problems. From having been dominated, the receptionists became integrators. To achieve customer-centricity, make the organization listen to those who listen to customers.

Changing interaction patterns among functions is much more powerful than creating a dedicated customer-centricity function.

At InterLodge, the management team took a work group that had an interest in cooperation and gave it the power to impel the cooperation of others. Sometimes, however, reinforcing integrators can involve reversing this dynamic: taking a work group with a lot of power that has typically *not* had an interest in cooperation and making changes that cause its members to develop such an interest. As we will see, this is what happened at MobiliTele.

MobiliTele: A Search for the Cause of Development Delays

When we first encountered MobiliTele, the company was taking more than thirty months to develop a new release of its network hardware and software. The industry benchmark was twenty. Because it took MobiliTele 50 percent more time to develop new products than their rivals, MobiliTele's profit margins and market share were declining while its defects were increasing. Only one of its operating groups, known as the transceiver unit, was able to deliver its work on time, on budget, and without defects. Faced with this poor performance, the company's executive team started to question the overall engagement of the various development units. So the team launched a survey to probe attitudes across four work groups:

- *Program managers* were responsible for overseeing the product development process and delivering new releases on time, providing technical specifications, setting project milestones, and monitoring the process across the engineering units that developed the three main components of the system.

- *The transceiver unit engineers* developed the transceiver, which receives and transmits the radio signal passing to and from cell phones on a network. (You have probably seen such devices mounted on towers and on top of buildings.)

- *Collector unit engineers* developed the technology that collects all the signals from the transceivers before they are dispatched to users across the network.

- *Software engineers* developed the software that operated and monitored the entire system.

As with most employee surveys, some questions addressed how people felt about the work processes involving other departments. When the engineers were asked about the program managers, the response was neutral. There weren't many complaints but not much positive feedback either (an unusual number of respondents marked "don't know"). The main impression was that the other units were indifferent to the project managers, their role, and their responsibilities. Their apathy suggested to us that the project managers weren't really functioning as integrators. As we said earlier, an integrator makes a difference for people, either positive or negative; therefore, people's relationship with integrators is always emotionally loaded. When you feel indifference for people, it is usually because they can't make a difference to you. (See the sidebar "Use Caution in Interpreting Emotions and Feelings at Work.")

Use Caution in Interpreting Emotions and Feelings at Work

When you observe strong emotions in the workplace, remember that they are the consequences and symptoms of behaviors. They may not mean what you think they do at first glance. For example:

- Tension between two work groups might be a symptom of a conflict so intense that it impedes cooperation. Alternatively, it might be a sign that people are doing the hard work of cooperation, with the tension arising from the adjustment costs they must bear.

- Good interpersonal relationships might be a sign that people feel that the adjustment costs of cooperation are worth it, given the individual benefit they are receiving. Alternatively, good relationships may be a sign that people are carefully avoiding cooperation in order not to accept or impose any costs of adjustment.

Don't assume you understand the meaning of strong emotions in the workplace context until you understand how those emotions are the result of behaviors shaped by a specific work context of goals, resources, and constraints.

Respondents expressed a great deal of resentment, however, toward the transceiver unit. According to managers, this resentment dated from when the company began to face tougher competition and the pressure to get out new releases had grown (before then, the three engineering units had all gotten along reasonably well). When we asked the transceiver engineers what they thought about the resentment, they replied, "Pure jealousy! It's because of our performance! We're the only group that gets its work done on time!"

In addition to these pseudo-psychological explanations ("jealousy!") coming from the members of the transceiver unit, some senior managers also offered cultural explanations to explain performance differences among the work units. The reason the transceiver unit was always on time and on budget? "They are best-in-class, always on time, very disciplined; of course, they're Swiss German!" (Indeed the transceiver unit was mainly located in Switzerland.)

Analyzing the Work Context at MobiliTele

We were not satisfied with these psychological and cultural explanations of what was happening at MobiliTele. So we began to analyze the work context, using the simple rule that we described in chapter 1.

The program managers were responsible for developing the overall product specifications. They did this by having conversations with their colleagues, including platform architects, members of the sales force, and marketing staff. They also spoke with their counterparts at the big mobile telephony operators that were MobiliTele's customers to develop an understanding of their needs.

The program managers then finalized the specs and communicated them to the engineering units. But even at this early stage, there were problems. Because the product releases were so far behind schedule, the specs for the next-generation release always arrived late as well. Indeed, the program managers had created a parallel schedule to the formal schedule that reflected these delays. The engineers in the three development groups had to report on both schedules, the formal one with its official milestones and deadlines, and the informal one that contained adjustments for the delays. Having become accustomed to the delay in the specs, however, the engineers had adjusted their behavior accordingly. Since they had a rough idea of what the next-generation product would be, they would start work on the development of their component before the final specs arrived. They patted themselves on the back for this exercise of initiative: "If we didn't get started early, the final product would be finished even later than it is."

Not all the engineering units were equally affected by the lateness of the product specs. The specs for the transceiver, it turned out, were largely determined by international communication standards and less so—in comparison to the other units—by clients, suppliers, or MobiliTele managers. As a result, the transceiver team could interpret what it thought the evolution of communication standards was going to be, start its work even earlier, and finish sooner than the other units.

This head start by the transceiver unit had a dramatic impact on the other development groups. The fact that the transceiver unit was always much further ahead than the other two units meant that, when the final specs arrived, the collector unit engineers and the software engineers had to develop the vast majority of workarounds and interfaces to ensure that their components were compatible with both the transceivers and the specs. That took additional time that was not in the schedule and additional money that was not in the budget. The later the final specs arrived, the more sense it made for the transceiver unit not to modify any of the work it had already done, and the greater the pressure on everyone else to modify theirs.

The negative effects of this dynamic went beyond the issue of delayed delivery. Constantly starting and then stopping to make fixes and workarounds to fit with what the transceiver unit had already done resulted in products that did not fully meet customers' needs and occasionally even led to product defects. When a customer complained, the platform architects and sales-people had to spend time explaining and justifying the changes, as well as negotiating rebates or other price adjustments. As a result, they had less time to work on preparing the product specs with program managers for the next generation of the product, which meant further delays. Because of all the workarounds and rework, we calculated that only 20 percent of the time the engineering teams spent on the development of any product actually added value.

Why People Do What They Do: Delays as a (Perverse) Resource

What was the real goal of the engineers? Was it to minimize delays? No. The engineering units were not penalized when the product was delivered late or even when it was defective. Still, delays meant having to anticipate what the next generation of specs would be, and anticipating invariably meant that they would have to do rework. So what was so great then about starting work before the specs arrived? Well, for one thing, the units could exercise maximum autonomy and organize around their own procedures and strengths. The more they leveraged their own resources, the more efficient they were, at least, as they were evaluated according to the criteria within their own unit.

What was their constraint then? Remember, constraints are what people avoid, sidestep, or try to minimize. By starting work early, engineers avoided the specs; these were their constraint. After all, the specs materialized and documented the interdependencies among the three development units. The real problem the engineers were trying to solve was how to cope with these complex interdependencies.

Starting early before the specs arrived (in order to save time) allowed the engineers to ignore some of these interdependencies. The longer the delay, the more justified each unit felt in taking unilateral action on what they anticipated the specs would be.

Was a delay a constraint, as you might assume? No, it was actually a resource, because it gave engineers a way out of the complex interdependencies. Even after the specs had arrived, the urgency and time pressure that the units experienced justified taking shortcuts and coming up with workarounds that also simplified critical dependencies. Of course, the delays functioned as a perverse resource, the kind that organizations often create unintentionally and that lead to poor performance.

The transceiver unit was best able to take advantage of this resource (the delays in the specs). Although its performance may have been best-in-class, the transceiver unit earned that distinction at the expense of the other units and of the overall organization (and it had nothing to do with the fact that the transceiver engineers happened to be Swiss). Rather, because the unit could get the biggest head start (due to the role of the international standards in transceiver design), it was in a position to force the other units to adjust in ways that degraded their performance in the form of workarounds that had not been budgeted up front. The greater the delays in the specs, the better the performance of the transceiver unit, compared with (and at the expense of) the rest of the organization.

Creating a New Constraint to Reinforce Integrators

How to reshape this dysfunctional work context? There was no doubt that the transceiver unit at MobiliTele held the power. It had the greatest influence on the issues that mattered to others. It could affect the amount of extra work the other units had to do and the technical difficulty involved. The development process's actual managers, the program managers, had no power. They represented an unnecessary overlay that had to be removed, along with its double-scheduling and reporting.

Since the transceiver unit had the power to force others to cooperate with it, we wondered, could the transceiver engineers perhaps be turned into genuine integrators? Could we create a situation in which they would have an interest to cooperate with and foster cooperation among the other product development units so that together they would make the optimal choices for the entire system? To do that, the transceiver unit would have to be made to bear the cost of its lack of cooperation with the other product development units.

So, we helped MobiliTele's management team create a new constraint for the transceiver unit: in the future, it was announced, the transceiver engineers would be accountable for any delay in the design and production of the *entire* system, not just the transceiver itself. They would accompany salespeople to review meetings at the telephony operators to hear their complaints about the functionality of MobiliTele's system, and it would be their responsibility to respond to any quality issues or concerns about missed deadlines. After spending a few marathon meetings listening to customers who were fed up with MobiliTele's constant delays and having to respond to difficult questions and come up with answers that satisfied the customers, the transceiver engineers definitely began to feel personally the costs of the insufficient cooperation among units.

The prospect of repeated exposure to interactions with unhappy customers had the effect of making cooperation individually beneficial for the transceiver engineers. Instead of just maximizing their own room for maneuver, they began to listen more to customers and to their marketing and sales colleagues and to discover ways of optimizing the interaction with their colleagues in the other product development units. This new context provided a way to make the transceiver engineers personally bear the cost of their uncooperative behaviors. So far they had been able to externalize that cost to other functions and third parties like customers and shareholders. Insufficient cooperation was now a constraint for the transceiver engineers, which not only led them to cooperate more with others but also to serve as effective integrators, expanding cooperation among the two other product development units, and allowing them to simplify the matrix structure by removing the program dimension. Internalizing the cost of insufficient cooperation onto those who generate them is a very effective way to promote cooperation.

Until recently, MobiliTele was a monopoly in some market segments. To realize the depth of the change it had to go through, we must go beyond the economic definition of a monopoly (one producer with many customers) and take an organizational sociology view. To be a monopoly means that an organization can make customers bear the cost of the comfortable avoidance of cooperation among its employees—in the form of delays, defects, and high prices. Because they have no choice, customers end up subsidizing the internal peace within the monopoly. With more intense competition as a result of deregulation, customers were now in a position to refuse to bear that cost. Real cooperation had to start at MobiliTele.

But the more work has relied on positive interpersonal feelings, the more a change at work will be experienced as a betrayal by those whose good feelings are strained by the change. This is what had happened at MobiliTele when its quasi-monopoly ended. The very social fabric of the company endured the friction inherent to cooperation, even if this cooperation had been insufficient (limited as it was to just making fixes within two units after the final specs arrived). This is why applying the first simple rule was so important: to show both managers and engineers that the real problem was not ill-will or jealousy, but the very functioning of the system. The systemic appraisal inherent to rule one helps depersonalize issues—showing that problems are not caused by the personal traits or hostility of people—and thus helps make change less personally difficult and dramatic.

At MobiliTele, the issue wasn't that the engineers didn't care or were cynically cheating their employer or were at fault for the problems in the company's product development process. They were trying hard to cope with the complexity of their interdependency. Remember, goals, resources, and constraints are not psychological concepts; they don't describe what people think. Rather, they describe the logic of people's behavior as actors in an organizational system. These concepts are meant to help you assess your organization from the perspective of the behaviors it indirectly shapes, instead of the perspective of the theoretical pros and cons supposed to be directly attached to certain kinds of structure, processes, systems, or personality traits.

After fifteen months, with the transceiver unit acting as integrator, the company was doing a much better job of satisfying its performance requirements. It was beating industry benchmarks for speed to market by 20 percent, while matching its competitors on cost and quality. There were no delays passed from one release to the next. The vicious circle had been broken.

Transforming Managers into Integrators

In an environment of complexity, being an integrator is—or, at least, ought to be—at the very heart of the managerial role. But in order to function effectively as integrators, managers must give up the assumptions of the hard and soft approach. People cannot be commanded to cooperate by forcing a new structure on them or coerced to do so with communications efforts or team-building exercises. People only cooperate when the context of work makes it individually useful for them to cooperate.

There are three things you can do to help your managers function as effective integrators—that is, instigators of productive cooperation for the good of the organization as a whole.

- **Remove managerial positions.** Some managerial roles will never have sufficient power to influence the work context so that people have an interest in cooperating. It's best to eliminate these positions.

- **Minimize rules.** Too many rules hem in managers and keep them from effectively exercising their judgment. It's best to minimize them.

- **Rely on judgment over metrics.** One of the paradoxes of cooperation is that it is extremely difficult to measure who contributes what. For managers to serve effectively as integrators, rely on their judgment instead of pseudo-precise metrics.

Limit Managerial Roles

Despite decades of delayering, most organizations continue to have more hierarchical layers than they need. These layers take many forms: project managers (like the ones at MobiliTele), dotted-line positions in matrix organizations, regional headquarters, and functional coordinators. Many of these layers are the inevitable result of the hard response to business complexity. But often another factor is also at play: because the company is not very good at inspiring people to perform, it creates new layers in order to offer promotions into managerial positions as a "carrot." These positions are just poor substitutes for genuine motivation; they don't add much value, and the roles have little or no power.

In companies that have hierarchies heavy with these coordinating functions and pseudo-managerial roles, there is such an excess of managers that they tend to lead very small teams, sometimes composed of only a few people. If a manager has only two direct reports, he or she depends 50 percent on each of them for the work that needs to be done. The reports, however, hardly depend on the manager at all. That's because, with so many layers and units, there are many ways to bypass the manager. The result is an inverted hierarchy: the manager depends more on the team than the team depends on the manager; managers have insufficient power to add value. It is better to have no hierarchy at all than an inverted hierarchy.

Therefore, the first step in reinforcing your managers to play the integrator role is to cut the number of hierarchical layers, which simultaneously increases the span of control and shortens hierarchical lines. When managers are too far from where the action takes place they need metrics, KPIs, and scorecards. All these are poor summaries and imprecise proxies for what people really do. These proxies fail to capture reality while also adding to complicatedness. Whereas most organizations think of delayering mainly in terms of cost savings, far more important is the way it can free up managers to really manage. When you remove a management layer that does not have sufficient power to actively shape people's work contexts, you not only eliminate an organizational element that is useless and adds to complicatedness (thus altering information and slowing down decisions). You also make it easier to reinforce as integrators the management layers that remain.

Keep and reinforce only those management positions for which you can give clear answers to these questions:

- What value is this managerial position supposed to add? What is this manager supposed to make teams do that the teams would not do spontaneously on their own? To be clear, we are not talking about writing a new job description. Answering such questions requires getting to the specifics about why you need this management layer and what would not happen without it. All too often, senior executives do not really know what value they expect their managers to add.

- Even when you are convinced that there is some value that managers can add to a particular task or work group, are you sure there is no other manager, located either below or above the work unit in the organization, who may be better placed to play the integrator role?

Minimize Rules

To be effective integrators, managers need room to maneuver so that they can make a difference for their teams. This freedom is often eaten away by procedural rules. Just as many organizations have too many layers of management, they also have far too many rules. As performance requirements multiply, they respond by multiplying procedures to address each requirement. When a new urgent need arises—to improve safety, reduce cost, or better manage risk, for example—the response is legislative, creating new formal rules. It's the same phenomenon that we see in government, where legislators respond to every call for action with a new law.

Rules in the workplace can take many different forms:

- *A process definition* specifies that the way to achieve X is by doing Y followed by Z.

- *A performance target* becomes a priority in every situation, even when the target doesn't really make sense.

- *A template* specifies the only way to convey a certain type of information.

- *Monitoring scorecards* specify how activity is recorded.

- *A computerized job request* is a rule on interaction.

- *An internal contract,* such as a service-level agreement (SLA) between support services and internal customers, details what mechanisms constitute minimum (and very often, therefore, maximum) service.

The overreliance on rules reflects a misunderstanding of how rules really function. It is not what the rule *decrees* that matters. It is the *effect* the rule has on the actions and interactions of the people involved—how the rule affects the context of goals, resources, and constraints to which people adjust their behaviors.

We have already discussed how rules are especially problematic for dealing with contradictory performance requirements. Rules cannot accommodate contradictions, but complexity is full of them. The imposition of formal guidelines meant to specify and control behaviors inevitably leads to one of two dead ends. First, the management team will create guidelines for each performance requirement, but, because the requirements are contradictory, the instructions will end up in conflict with one another, leading to confusion and often considerable stress (dealing with a complex problem is one thing; working with contradictory orders for how to go about the task is quite another).

Alternatively, the management team will create a rule that specifies the trade-offs between contradictory performance requirements. But a trade-off specified in advance will always be at some distance from the situation-specific optimum that can be found in the here and now. That distance was not necessarily an issue when customers had few options to choose from. But in the current business environment where choices abound, the sum of such distances—mounting up day after day, situation after situation—is what separates winners from losers. No set of instructions can ever be complete, current, or flexible enough to bend around the numerous, changing, and contradictory needs that arise in the workplace. Only when people use their judgment and the information at their disposal can they deal with the contradictions contained in complex situations.

But there is another problem with an overreliance on procedural rules if managers are to function as integrators. Beyond a certain threshold (which can only be determined by the specific work context), adding new rules also decreases management's control over the people to whom the rules apply. Indeed, it's no coincidence that one of the most effective practices of labor unions is the so-called "work to rule" action in which, instead of going on strike, workers instead adhere strictly to every rule, to the degree that no real work can get done.

No matter how carefully a rule is devised, it will always require some judgment and interpretation in execution. But by definition, there can be no rule about how to correctly interpret a rule. People need to determine the spirit of the rule beyond its letter. They must use their intelligence within each situation, instead of just checking the box.[1] Therefore, the more rules there are, the more managers depend on the good will of the team members in interpreting the rules. The real issue with too many rules is not that they constrain freedom, but that they create freedom in a system designed to avoid it—in a system thus unable to orient people's freedom so that it serves the ultimate goals of the organization.

As the rules pile up and apply to more practices, managers can make less of a difference for their teams. They do not have the power to make or change the rules, because rule-making power is typically held at the top of the organization or by authoritative bodies, such as regulators or unions. The result is, again, an inverted hierarchy. Managers increasingly depend on their teams, and teams depend less and less on their managers.

This counterintuitive effect of rules explains why requests for more rules often come from the team members, rather than from their manager. Rules protect teams from the hierarchy by diminishing managers' room to maneuver. Midlevel and field managers, in particular, get squeezed between the top-down demand for control and the bottom-up desire for protection. Gradually, people at both the top and the bottom of the organization become distrustful of the managers in the middle who seem unable to ensure effective performance, despite the abundance of rules that supposedly gives them power to control but, in fact, takes it away from them.

So, to reinforce your managers as effective integrators, make sure they are bound by fewer rules. That way, they will be free to use their judgment in setting targets and articulating ambitions, in defining success criteria, and in evaluating and rewarding performance. The same is true of a company as it grows. The bigger a company gets, the greater its need for integrators and, therefore, the more it needs to remove rather than add rules. But companies more frequently do the opposite. (See the sidebar "The Benefits of Reinforcing Integrators.")

The Benefits of Reinforcing Integrators

- More direct cooperation to optimize contradictory performance requirements.

- Less complicatedness thanks to the removal of matrix dimensions and hierarchical layers.

- Less waste and fewer mistakes that result from escalating decisions.

- Decisions made as close as possible to where the action takes place and where information is richest.

Rely on Judgment over Metrics

Another counterproductive effect of the hard approach is that it leads managers to rely mainly on measurement to know whom they must reward. Careful measurement supposedly serves accuracy, objectivity, and thus performance. But too much reliance on metrics to assess and reward individual performance can actually become a detriment to performance because it impedes managers' ability to act as integrators.

When all the people involved in a task cooperate, their individual efforts combine instead of being simply additive. This compounding of effort makes a great difference to team performance. When people cooperate in this way, however, some portion of their individual effort manifests itself only in the achievements of others. It becomes impossible to measure who contributed what to the overall performance of the group.[2] In a 4 × 100 meter relay race, for example, the victorious team is not always the one that has the fastest sprinters. The runners also have to skillfully pass the baton. To do so, they must divert energy to their arms to properly make the pass and to their voices to effectively communicate—rather than putting all their energy into their legs for maximum speed. Consider the 2003 World Athletics Championships. Of the eight teams competing in the women's 4 × 100 meter relay final, the United States was heavily favored yet the French team won. Based on the individual records of its runners, the US team should have been the fastest by far. The sum of the 100-meter personal best performances of the four US runners, compared to that of the French runners, gave the US team an edge of as much as 3.2 meters. And, considering 2003 performances only, the US margin over their French rivals was 6.4 meters. According to Christine Arron, who ran the final leg for the French, the win was achieved through exceptional cooperation.[3] In this kind of activity, there is no way to precisely measure individual performance. Did one sprinter run a particularly fast individual leg? Or, was her exceptional performance a consequence of the previous sprinter transferring the baton especially smoothly? No metric will provide the answer. The energy in one runner's arm in passing the baton makes a difference in the speed of the next runner's legs—but how much? (See the sidebar "Cooperation Cannot Be Measured.")

To cooperate always involves a decision about how to allocate your efforts, time, and energy. That decision always carries some degree of personal risk. You agree to sacrifice the ultimate

---

KEEP IN MIND

Cooperation Cannot Be Measured

What you can measure:

- Overall group output (revenues, profit, return on investment, speed to market, and so on).

- Some individual inputs (efficiency of units in tasks independent of others).

What you can't accurately measure:

- The contribution of one individual or unit to the effectiveness of others (the contribution of procurement to the effectiveness of manufacturing, the contribution of front offices to the effectiveness of back offices, and so on).

Therefore:

- Don't measure behavior; measure results.

- Use judgment rather than measurements to evaluate the degree of cooperation.

---

protection granted by your measurable performance in order to enhance in a disproportionate way the performance of others and the overall results.

When companies only use individual KPIs to reward performance, people put all their energy into the individual output that can be measured, at the expense of cooperation and group results. But collective goals don't do the trick either. They are necessary, but insufficient. Unless cooperation also makes a difference to the individual, he or she will stop taking the risk to cooperate with others. (We will come back to this issue in chapter 4 when we discuss rich objectives.)

Yes, companies need measurement, and they should measure whatever is useful and measurable to monitor performance. But in order to foster cooperation, they must move beyond KPIs and other formal systems for appraisal. Since cooperation cannot be measured, rewarding people for their cooperation can only come through the personal recognition of the manager. Such recognition is the product, not of metrics, but of observation and judgment. As the word suggests, *recognition* is about *cognition*, knowing what people do and understanding what is really going on.

This imperative sheds some fresh light on the necessary linkages between our first two simple rules. Many discussions about leadership emphasize the importance of managerial presence in the workplace. By now, you should realize that this presence is not some empty slogan or abstract philosophical stance. It is an extremely practical issue: managers need to be present to observe and gather, through conversation and interactions, the nonmeasurable data that reveals the content and result of cooperation. This is what social sciences demonstrate and what great managers do. Sir Alex Ferguson, the outstanding former manager of Manchester United, the English football (soccer) club, put it this way: "I don't think many people fully understand the value of observing. I came to see observation as a critical part of my management skills."[4] In the financial industry, catastrophes could have been avoided if some managers had applied the observation principle. This kind of in-depth knowledge of the work context has nothing to do with what some call "micromanagement." The goal is not to be constantly telling people what to do but, rather, to use this in-depth knowledge to continually shape and reshape the work context to foster cooperation. Only when they do so can managers function effectively as integrators.

SUMMARY OF SIMPLE RULE TWO

Reinforce integrators by looking at those directly involved in the work, giving them power and interest to foster cooperation in dealing with complexity instead of resorting to the paraphernalia of overarching hierarchies, overlays, dedicated interfaces, balanced scorecards, or coordination procedures.

- Among operational units, find those that can play the role of integrators among peer units, because of some particular interest or power.

- Use feelings to identify candidates: feelings provide important clues for the analysis, because they are symptoms rather than causes.

- Among managerial layers, remove those who cannot add value and reinforce others as integrators by eliminating some rules and relying on observation and judgment rather than metrics whenever cooperation is involved.

3

Simple Rule Three

Increase the Total Quantity of Power

The more an organization needs cooperation to address complexity, the more power you need to have in the organization. In the previous chapter, we discussed the importance of power in reinforcing the role of the integrator, for instance, the empowerment of InterLodge's receptionists and the vesting of interest in the MobiliTele transceiver unit. Now, we must draw a distinction between simply redistributing power (as was the case at InterLodge) and actually increasing the total quantity of power in the organization. In this chapter, we will discuss how to increase the total quantity of power available and why it is so important in today's business environment.

You will learn:

- **How to understand power.** Power is not a direct function of position, individual skills, or authority. Rather, it derives from the possibility for one person to make a difference on issues that matter to someone else.

- **How to create new sources of power.** By increasing the amount of power available in the organization, more people will take the risk to cooperate.

- **How to use power skillfully** for better strategy, leadership, and organizational design, thus achieving performance levels beyond the reach of traditional solutions.

We will illustrate these lessons through the story of a company we call GrandeMart, which solved a performance problem by giving local store managers a new source of power.

What Power Is—and What It Isn't

Most managers understand that power is an important part of organizational life. But their understanding is often corrupted by the assumptions embedded in the hard and soft approaches. The hard approach assumes that power is an automatic consequence of position or formal authority. This belief is reflected in comments such as "the higher you are on the org chart, the more power you have," or "if you have the authority, you automatically have the power," or "if you have the knowledge, you have the power."

The soft approach, by contrast, tends to focus on leadership style or personal traits such as charisma. This view is reflected in statements such as "she is a tremendously powerful person" or "he has a presence that projects power."

Power is none of these things. Overly complicated organizations have managers in all kinds of positions that, according to the org chart, have authority, but who in reality have little or no power to make things happen. (See the sidebar "Three Myths about Power.")

These misunderstandings about power did not do much harm when relatively few interactions were required to get things done, say, on the traditional assembly line. But the more that performance requires multiple interactions among many different

KEEP IN MIND

Three Myths about Power

- *Power is an attribute of position.* This statement is not true; reporting lines—whether full, dotted, or bold—are just formal conventions without any automatic effect.

- *Authority is equivalent to power.* This statement is also not true; authority provides the legitimacy to exercise power, not power itself.

- *Power is an attribute of individuals and their leadership style.* Again, this statement is not true; personal attributes or style may be ways to exercise power but don't determine whether an individual has power in the first place.

organizational units, the more these common misunderstandings about power become costly for the company and its people.

What *is* power? Power is the possibility for one person to make a difference on issues—or stakes—that matter to someone else. Because *A* can make a difference on issues that matter to *B*, then *B* will do things that he or she would not have done without *A*'s intervention. Power always exists, one way or another, either helping or hindering good outcomes. It helps mobilize people, either directly or indirectly, toward a specific target or a goal. Look to the places in an organization where people are doing things that if, left to their own devices, they probably would not be doing. It is a sure bet that someone is exercising power over them.

Another way of putting it is that power comes from having control over uncertainties that are relevant to others and to the organization. The control of uncertainties determines the terms of exchange between the individual and the organization. The greater the uncertainties controlled by one actor for other organization members, the better that actor can negotiate his or her participation and the more he or she will get in return from the organization. This insight is a major contribution from the strategic analysis method developed by Michel Crozier and Erhard Friedberg.[1] Think back to the transceiver engineers at MobiliTele. Because they were able to set de facto specifications for the transceiver and the other components of the system— determining how much rework engineers in the other units would have to do—they controlled a key uncertainty for those units. As a result, the transceiver engineers could organize around their own priorities, and other units had to adjust and bear the consequences.

As this example suggests, power exists only in the relations between people; it is an imbalanced exchange of behaviors. Despite popular belief, power is not particularly related to an imbalance of information available to the parties. Instead, the asymmetry relates to the terms of exchange in a relationship: the reciprocal possibilities of action. The imbalance—thus, the power—comes from the fact that A can make a greater difference regarding stakes that matter to B than the reverse. On another issue or as the stakes change, though, B may have power over A. Power is an attribute neither of position nor of people's personality traits. Rather, it stems from a relationship tied to a situation.

Power has significant implications for how behaviors adjust to each other. The people with the most power bear the least adjustment cost; those with the least power bear the most. The powerless will adjust their behavior to the powerful. Depending on how these behaviors adjust and combine with each other, the results will be more or less beneficial for performance. If what is ideal for the powerful deviates from the company's overall goals, the power balance will not be beneficial to the company. That was the case with the powerful transceiver unit at MobiliTele; what was ideal for the unit had a negative impact on the company's ability to bring superior products to market quickly.

Why Increasing the Total Quantity of Power Is So Important

When power is used to mobilize collective action that furthers the goals of an organization, it is a fabulous thing. This is what happened at InterLodge, as we saw in chapter 2. When the hotel receptionists were given more power (in the form of a voice in the performance evaluation of maintenance and housekeeping staff), they had much greater capacity to play the integrator role. The end result was more—and more effective—cooperation in the achievement of the organization's goals.

What happened at InterLodge is what people in the business world often call "empowerment." It involved a redistribution of power from the back-office functions to the receptionists. In the past, promotion within the back-office functions of maintenance and housekeeping was determined exclusively by the managers of those functions. By giving the receptionists a say in back-office performance evaluations and promotion decisions, InterLodge management shifted some of that power to the receptionists.

As effective as such reallocations of power can be, however, it is increasingly important in situations of business complexity for organizations to create many *new* sources of power. Coping with complexity requires higher levels of both autonomy and cooperation. But when people cooperate, they are no longer self-sufficient; they become dependent on others. Therefore, the influence you have (or do not have) over others will play a central role in your decision not only to cooperate but also how much to cooperate. The more influence you have over the behavior of others, the more you can take the risk of becoming dependent on what they do. In other words, power determines the capacity to enter into the kind of cooperative interactions and reciprocity of action that are essential for addressing business complexity.

For this reason, power in the organization often needs to be something more than a zero-sum game. If power is only redistributed, then as performance requirements multiply, there will always be someone without the power to step into the cooperation game. The day InterLodge needed to offer innovative new services (Internet connectivity) to its customers, the organization had to create new power bases for its maintenance staff.

You need to create a positive-sum game. You need to increase the total quantity of power in the organization so that the power given to some does not come at the expense of the power of others. The new power can benefit managers in their integrator role and also team members so they can further cooperate with others. That way, you can channel the intelligence of more people against more fronts in a coherent yet flexible way, for both greater effectiveness and adaptiveness.

The Manager's Role in Increasing Power: Creating New Stakes

Given that power is so important to success in the modern business organization, a key role of the manager is to find ways to create new sources of power and to multiply the power bases inside the organization. He or she can do so by adding at least one new stake that matters to someone and that the achievement of which depends on others in the organization. A stake is something that matters to people, that makes a difference to them. A stake can be either positive or negative, something that a particular individual or group either wants to have or wants to avoid. Those who have an influence over this stake will benefit from having power over those for whom the stake matters. When a stake is new, it is a new power base that benefits some without being taken away from others.

Of course, not all stakes will create the kind of power that will mobilize action in the direction the organization needs and wants. A stake that is meaningful to an individual or group but has no relation to the performance requirements of the organization is obviously not an appropriate or effective stake. Rather, managers need to come up with stakes that matter to the relevant actors and also relate positively to the company's performance requirements.

To illustrate these concepts, let us consider the example of GrandeMart, a large retailer, and how we used a simple intervention to create new power and thus improve performance.

GrandeMart: Managers Need to Add Value but Have Lost Power

Over a decade, the retailer had lost ground on two fronts: to discounters that successfully undercut GrandeMart on price and to specialty stores that offered better selection and higher quality in specific categories of goods. The company's market share was being eaten away, and it was losing sales and foot traffic every year.

GrandeMart decided that, in order to regain market share, it had to find ways to adapt its stores to the greater diversity of local consumption patterns and preferences. The change in GrandeMart's customer profiles had been particularly dramatic. In one major city, for example, GrandeMart stores in three different city locations now served very different customers. Ten years earlier, the customers in all three localities had fit roughly the same profile. As part of this plan to diversify the company's stores and localize the offering, the senior management team directed each store to hold a monthly sale or promotion featuring products that would be of particular appeal to local customers. Each month, every store would reconfigure its layout, refresh its displays, and hold events that related to the theme of that particular month.

To do all this required a good deal of diligence and responsiveness on the part of the store employees. They also had to cooperate across departments (such as grocery, personal care, home goods, and others) within the store. The store managers had to mobilize the efforts of their teams, getting them all to work in sync.

Therein lay the problem. Although they held positions of authority, the store managers at GrandeMart did not have much power, not much influence on issues that mattered to their employees. Over the years, as the market had changed, the company, like many others, had centralized its key functions in order to benefit from economies of scale. As a result, the store managers could no longer make much of a difference for their employees. All the major issues that matter in the day-to-day life of employees in the stores—about their product assortment, product availability, and prices, and about human resource management policies and systems—were decided at the center. The managers had become little more than "nice nannies," as one employee put it. Remember the managers we described in chapter 1 who complained about all their administrative tasks and yet spent most of their time working on them? These were the store managers at GrandeMart. As a result, they avoided launching the monthly promotional campaigns; they were adjusting their goals and aspirations to the poor resources granted by the very limited power they had to mobilize the teams.

GrandeMart couldn't give back to the store managers the influence on assortment, procurement, prices, policies, and systems they had lost over the years. The competitive requirements for consistency and economies of scale had not disappeared. How could a new source of power be created in the stores to allow them to effectively mobilize their teams in the localization initiative, without compromising on the other requirements?

Creating a New Base of Power

The challenge was finding some stake that had three characteristics:

- *It mattered to the company* as a whole, because it affected how it would meet its performance requirements.

- *It mattered to the store departments,* because it pertained to an uncertainty that affected what they had to do in particular situations.

- *It was controlled by store managers.* It was important that the store managers had the possibility to make a difference on the stake, which would increase their power such that they could mobilize store employees to meet the new demands of localization.

The stake we identified related to an important performance requirement: improving customer satisfaction, notably when it came to the amount of time customers had to wait in the checkout line. The waiting time at checkout was a key determinant of a customer's in-store experience. It had a significant impact on customer loyalty and the frequency of visits to the store.

The longer the lines, the less often customers came to the store. Some customers, seeing how long the lines were, would head back to their cars and leave. In a major communication campaign, GrandeMart announced that in order to better serve its customers, the lines at the checkout stations would never get too long. The company even marked on the floor of some stores just exactly what "too long" meant.

To keep this new commitment, senior management decided that whenever the lines at the checkout stations got too long, new stations would open immediately. To open more checkout stations, however, would require that employees from other departments would be assigned to operate the stations. This new practice gave us the opening we needed. Here was a stake that clearly mattered to organizational performance but also mattered a great deal to employees across the entire store.

How store employees felt about suddenly being directed to help at checkout depended on their immediate work situation. When it forced them to interrupt a task they were engaged in or to confront annoyed and irritated customers, fed up from waiting in lines, the employees experienced it as a major disruption of their day. In those situations, however, when having to help at checkout freed them from a task they did not particularly enjoy, they appreciated it as a welcome diversion. We all have tasks we prefer to others, and it also depends on circumstances.

Our idea was to have the store managers decide which employees would be called away from their departments to fill in at the overflow checkout stations. We didn't develop any elaborate criteria or rules for deciding whom they should choose. We left it up to their judgment. Our goal was to give them a new source of power that would provide them with leverage in the larger task of mobilizing the departments for the monthly localization campaign.

At first glance, letting the store managers decide who had to work at the extra checkout stations at moments of high customer demand might seem like a trivial change. It certainly didn't require any major structural changes or the usual hard or soft initiatives. Yet, when you think about it, this simple change had enormous leverage. Store managers now could make a difference that mattered to their employees, and that mattered for performance. Adding value and having power are the two sides of the same coin in effective organizations. When it comes to designing organizations, it is helpful to consider the power perspective. Store employees now had something to gain from listening to the priorities set by the store manager—being assigned to the checkout counter only when they wanted to be. Of course, it was not an explicit negotiation—"If you do a good job working with others on the special events, I'll take it into account when I have to assign people to checkout"—but it was clear enough to give store managers a new card in the game.

Employee behavior began to shift. They started to listen to the store managers and take their needs and priorities into account. They engaged more with the store managers in developing ideas for customizing store offerings and monthly special events. They were more willing to cooperate with people in other departments on these events.

The increased cooperation in the stores also had some powerful second-order effects. The first concerned the special monthly promotions. In the past, they had been a constraint for store managers, so much so that the managers actually avoided launching them. But now that they could better mobilize their people, these events became a resource and they put their full energy behind them. The events provided even more opportunities to make a difference, yet more cards in the game.

By increasing the total quantity of power, GrandeMart was able to maintain its necessary consistency and economies of scale at the center, while also providing store managers with the power needed to implement customized improvements in local store operations. As a result of these endeavors, sales increased by multiple percentage points in the stores that applied the new approach, with an equivalent increase in foot traffic, reversing the previous decline in both measures.

But there was another second-order benefit: better cooperation between central functions and store managers. The functional managers at GrandeMart's corporate center regularly designed performance improvement initiatives that they would roll out across the stores. In the past, interactions between functions and stores had been limited to defining the road map and milestones to implement the performance initiatives. Now that the managers' context had changed, they could also make a greater difference for the functional managers by mobilizing their teams in support of a new improvement initiative.

The store managers now controlled a key uncertainty for the central functions. Therefore it was genuinely in the interests of the central functions to even more deeply listen to the store managers and to take into account their suggestions so that, in return, the store managers would effectively mobilize their teams on the center's initiatives. This new power vis-à-vis the functional managers created a situation in which the store managers could also take the risk to further cooperate with the central functions—for instance by being more transparent about their store's improvement potential. Beyond coordinating timelines, functions and stores could engage in a richer joint exploration of performance improvement opportunities. Store managers engaged even more actively in the initiatives launched by the center, leading to further improvement in performance. Store managers and their teams had become more effective players in the organizational system, and the organization was now able to more fully leverage their intelligence and judgment.

Power as a Positive-Sum Game

As the GrandeMart story suggests, turning power into a positive-sum game is like increasing the number of cards in the deck. The more cards in the deck, the greater the variety of moves each player can make. In the workplace, the greater the quantity of power available, the more initiatives individuals or units can take with others, the more willing they will be to accept transparency about their performance, and the more likely they are to participate—without limiting the participation of others.

By calling on organizations to increase the total quantity of power, we are not suggesting that every single organizational unit has to have exactly the same amount. It is not necessary (or possible) to even out power across all contexts and eventualities so that every entity is always equal in the amount of power it has over others. We are suggesting, however, that it is critical to avoid an overconcentration of power that causes others to withdraw from cooperation. When some players are dominated by others, they tend to isolate themselves. Below a certain threshold of cards in their hands, and whenever they have a choice, people are better off avoiding cooperation as they would bear most of the adjustment costs. Only those players who can act on a problem critical for others—who control a relevant uncertainty—will find room in the exchange relationship that underlies cooperation.

When creating new bases of power for people who have heretofore been dominated players in the organization, it's important to determine the critical mass of new power that will really make a difference. Sometimes, we hear executives say, "Our managers are given the power to evaluate performance fairly, thanks to our new evaluation system. But they don't use their power. They give everybody high marks even when it's obvious that performance is not as good as it should be." We also frequently hear that managers are provided with new levers to manage their team, but "lack the courage" to put the levers to use. This type of judgment is typical of the pseudo-psychology of the soft approach. What it usually means is that people have some authority (over some decisions) but not real power. It's a bit like the soldier facing ten enemies with only one bullet in his gun. In such a situation, the gun isn't a resource; it's a constraint.[2] Using the gun exposes the soldier to more problems than it solves.

When you create power, there has to be enough of it to be used. If the power falls short of this threshold, it is not a resource; it is a constraint. This is why managers do not use the power they are given, because it is not enough to make a difference. Suppose the manager uses the new evaluation system and gives a bad grade to a poor performer. That person responds, "I'm very disappointed. I feel demotivated. Maybe I could go on a training course to improve?" But suppose the manager does not have any training resources. The result is that the manager will have to deny the request and may not be able to count on his team member's engagement.

The only way you will know whether people have a critical mass of power—enough to use it—is by applying the first simple rule: understand what your people actually do and why they do it. In the case of middle managers, ask yourself these questions:

- What levers are at their disposal—in terms of budgeting, staffing, target setting, evaluating performance, influencing those issues that matter to teams? What room for maneuver do they have in using these levers?

- What would happen to managers if they were to use these levers? Are these levers resources or constraints for them?

- Have you created the right context of goals, resources, and constraints in which using these levers in an effective way is an individually useful behavior (rational strategy) for these managers?

Harnessing Power to Face Complexity

Being able to increase the total quantity of power available in the organization allows managers to think about and act on more performance requirements. This has implications for strategy and leadership. It also has implications for organization design.

Strategy and Leadership to Keep Pace with Complexity

Performance requirements have become both numerous and contradictory. Every time a new requirement emerges, a new degree of freedom is created for players to gain or lose customers and thus market positions. This complexity creates new volatility. Indeed, each additional performance requirement creates a new opportunity for competitors to make a difference vis-à-vis each other. This is one of the main reasons why market leadership volatility—measured by the frequency of changes in market share positions among competitors—has multiplied by a factor of twenty-two since the 1950s.[3] Because of this volatility, strategy is less a matter of positions—having strongholds in this or that domain—and more a matter of quickly adapting to opportunities as they arise. Competitive advantage is a matter of agility and adaptation, requiring the organization to nurture more options.

The third simple rule is the cornerstone of building such options: enriching the system by growing the realm of opportunities. Only when there are people with power can a company build new capabilities. Companies that increase the total quantity of power have widened their range of possible strategic moves. As French military strategist General André Beaufre pointed out, the very essence of strategy is protecting and increasing freedom for action.[4] The organization is not just in the service of executing the strategy; rather, it is what determines the very possibility of a strategy.

However, leading such a high-powered, highly adaptive organization poses new challenges. Leaders in such organizations need to be constantly on the lookout for ways to increase the number of stakes that are meaningful to people and also important to the performance requirements. They need to be closely in touch with the needs and goals of their people and to understand what really matters to them. They need to understand what people really do.

Integrating Power in Organizational Design

In the hard and soft approaches, power is the missing element in organizational design. When organizational design focuses exclusively on structure and processes, the result is often what we call a pendulum effect in which power swings back and forth from one group to another, often with destabilizing effects.

Take the example of the different organizational design solutions to the inevitable tension between line managers and project managers. Starting in the 1980s, many companies introduced a new role—the project manager—to improve their product development and customer-service capabilities. This evolution made the matrix structure much more common. The goal of the project manager role was to get teams composed of members from many different line departments (marketing, design, engineering, manufacturing, sales, and sourcing) to cooperate on the development of new products so that they would be completed on spec, on budget, and on time, or better serving important customers so that the company maximized its profitable sales.

To do this effectively, project managers needed power, and organizations gave it to them. They got the power to evaluate team members, which had traditionally been the role of the line manager, and have some say in rewards and promotions. But this power came at the expense of the line managers. As a result, the line managers became less able to mobilize their people when it came to achieving line objectives, such as building new capabilities or deploying new technological standards. These companies improved significantly in terms of meeting short-term project goals, but at the cost of seriously degrading their performance when it came to longer-term goals such as maintaining and extending the experience base of the workforce or engaging in cutting-edge technological innovation.

When companies facing this dilemma began to realize that they were losing ground on the long-term targets, they then embarked on yet another redesign to reempower line managers. But, of course, this new power shift often came at the expense of short-term performance on projects. So the pendulum kept swinging, each time disrupting the business and disorienting people and without these companies being able to reconcile their short- and long-term requirements.

Matrix organizations are not always necessary, but no matrix can succeed without increasing the total quantity of power so that everyone has enough power to achieve his or her objectives. One company made the pendulum stop swinging by creating a new stake controlled by line managers. The new stake was career progression for engineers based on expertise. Line managers became responsible for assessing engineers on a variety of specific skills and could move high scorers into expert positions. This responsibility was a new card in the game, which went into the line managers' hands. It also related to an important performance imperative for the company: competence development. Both line and project managers now have the power they need to mobilize teams on both short- and longer-term objectives.

Another example of the pendulum effect in organizational design is the age-old debate about centralization versus decentralization. For decades, local managers controlled many company decisions—including advertising, manufacturing, buying, recruitment, and promotions. In banks, for example, branch managers made the most critical decisions; in pharmaceuticals, it was the country managers.

Then, about twenty years ago, everything began to change. Shifting trade barriers provided an opportunity to leverage economies of scale, and technological innovation provided new ways to do it. Companies centralized functions and standardized processes. The local managers found themselves with very little power. This is what had happened to GrandeMart's store managers. Decisions about personnel, product selection, and supplier relationships were all handled centrally. In pharmaceuticals, the heads of country operations often were reduced to little more than acting as points of contact on local regulatory issues.

More recently, however, everything has changed again. Global markets have become more volatile and demanding. As a result, companies need to respond to local conditions and adapt to local demands. They need to add new capabilities to their local operations to ensure responsiveness, adaptability, and customization.

Many companies have again decentralized some activities but often at the expense of other requirements, triggering another swing of recentralization. Such pendulum shifts not only fail to satisfy the various performance requirements, but also add the disruption of frequent structural changes. The only solution is to create new power bases at the local level—at stores, branches, and countries—thus achieving both economies of scale and local responsiveness. Then companies reconcile what centralization and decentralization aim at, which no structural solution can achieve.

Again, this costly and ineffective back-and-forth organizational design is driven by a belief in the intrinsic effect of structure. But the effect of structure is conditional and indirect:

- It is conditioned by the other organizational elements with which structures combine.

- It is indirect because what matters is not the elements (whether considered in themselves according to their supposed pros and cons, or considered according to their mutual consistency), but how their combination shapes the goals, resources, and constraints to which people adjust their conducts.

It's possible to stop the pendulum swing between line management and project management or between centralization and decentralization. But it requires putting a rigorous consideration

SIMPLE RULES TOOLKIT

Organizational Design: Thinking beyond Structure, Process, and Systems

Don't think of organizational design in terms of structures, processes, and systems. *Do we have the right structure? Should we organize by customer segments, geographies, or functions? Should we go for parallel or sequential processes?* Since each of these solutions is supposed to carry intrinsic benefits to deal with specific performance requirements, you will end up with an n-dimensional matrix organization—by region, product, function, segment, etc.—as there are more and more requirements to satisfy.

Instead, think of organizational design in terms of power bases and the resulting capabilities. Capabilities are concrete behaviors, embedded in people with power and interest to do something. *What do we want our organization to be able to do tomorrow that it can't do today? Who needs to have power to achieve these goals and how will we provide it to them?*

of power at the very center of organizational design. (See the sidebar "Organizational Design.")

Here are a few power-related issues to consider when making your design decisions:

- Identify the stakes that matter for organizational members. Is it staffing on this or that project, working with this or that technology, the allocation of tasks within teams, control of work flow, working times, promotion, or geographic mobility?

- Identify the people who control these stakes, how many they control, and their goals and problems.

- Assess if there is an overconcentration of power that hinders the full participation of those whose work has an impact on the multiple requirements of performance.

- Make sure each function has the power it needs and create new power bases accordingly.

The kinds of changes that companies make when applying simple rule three—such as giving a store manager the power for key staffing decisions—often look small in comparison to major structural changes. But structural changes alone can't take into account systemic effects such as power and cooperation, so they often do not have the positive effect on performance that smaller changes do. Of course, the resource of power is necessary but insufficient to ensure cooperation for the good of the company. For cooperation to be beneficial, you also need some constraints. This is where simple rules four, five, and six come into play.

SUMMARY OF SIMPLE RULE THREE

Whenever you consider an addition to your organization's structure, processes, and systems, think about increasing the quantity of power. Doing so may save you from increasing complicatedness and enable you to achieve greater impact with less cost. This can be done by enabling some functions to have an influence on new stakes that matter to others and performance.

- Whenever you are going to make a design decision that will swing the pendulum—between center and units, between functions and line managers, and so on—see if making some parts of the organization benefit from new power bases could, in fact, satisfy more requirements in dealing with complexity so that you don't have to swing the pendulum in the other direction in the future (which would only compound complicatedness with the mechanical frictions and disruptions inherent to these changes).

- When you have to create new functions, make sure you give them the power to play their role, and that this power does not come at the expense of the power needed by others to play theirs.

- When you create new tools for managers (planning, or evaluation systems, for instance), ask yourself if these constitute resources or constraints. Providing a few tools simultaneously is more effective (because it creates a critical mass of power) than many tools in a sequential way, one after the other.

- Regularly enrich power bases to ensure agility, flexibility, and adaptiveness.

4

Simple Rule Four

Increase Reciprocity

How can you ensure that an organization channels each person's autonomy in the most effective way? The three simple rules we described in the previous chapters improve people's ability to deal with complexity—the multiple, fast-changing, and often contradictory performance requirements companies need to satisfy. These rules provide people with new resources—knowledge of others and their work contexts, integrators that help foster the cooperation of others, and new sources of power—so they are able to make better decisions and take effective action. Put another way, these rules are about using the group to leverage people's autonomy. Their effect is to enhance the *potential* of the individual's judgment and energy.

In the next three chapters, we will describe the simple rules that impel people to deal with complexity. These three rules channel people's enhanced judgment and energy so that they actually *do* make better decisions and take actions that improve overall performance. These rules are about putting each individual's autonomy in the service of the group. Their effect is to ensure that people's enhanced potential achieved by the first three rules is *fully* used for the good of the company.

The last three rules achieve this by creating feedback loops that expose people, as directly as possible, to the consequences of their actions. Some of these feedback loops are contained in tasks and activities, rather than imposed from outside, so they have an immediate effect on people—either gratifying or penalizing—depending on how much good they do in their current work situations. The use of direct feedback loops leads to greater flexibility and adaptiveness in organizations, because the loops tailor themselves to specific circumstances. The more direct the feedback loops you create, the better you will meet your performance requirements and the more organizational complicatedness you can avoid.

The fourth simple rule—increase reciprocity—creates a context in which each person's success comes to depend on the personal success of others, just as overall performance depends on cooperation among individuals or groups. By reciprocity, we mean the recognition on the part of an organization's members that they have a mutual interest in cooperation—that the success of one depends on the success of all. By applying this rule, the technical and economic interdependencies of the tasks involved in performance are reflected in the personal interdependencies between people, because of the mutual interests at stake. The primary management tool for increasing reciprocity is the design of what we term *rich objectives*.

In this chapter, you will learn:

- **How the hard approach to the design of roles and objectives actually destroys a sense of reciprocity.** Just as conventional views of power can lead to counterproductive zero-sum power shifts and the pendulum effect, there are common misconceptions about roles and objectives that make it more difficult—and sometimes impossible—for people to recognize a mutual interest in cooperation.

- **How to design rich objectives.** Rich objectives help organizations increase reciprocity. They are composed of three elements: collective output objectives, individual input objectives, and overlap objectives. Together, these elements make interdependencies more visible to people, so they recognize the need for reciprocity.

- **How to change the context to reinforce rich objectives.** There are three steps companies can take to reinforce rich objectives: eliminate internal monopolies, remove resources that fuel dysfunctional self-sufficiency, and create multiple networks of interaction (what we call *multiplexity*). These steps intensify the interdependencies in the organization so that people are compelled to take them into account, that is, to cooperate.

To help illustrate these points, we will tell the story of an industrial goods company we call Industronal that was under intense competitive pressure to improve the quality of its products. We will describe how rich objectives helped the company's purchasing function cope with the necessity of cutting purchasing costs by 20 percent without compromising on quality and on-time delivery of supplies to internal end users.

Three Misconceptions about Roles and Objectives

Before we dive into the Industronal story, we'll address three misconceptions about how to define employees' roles and objectives that have their origins in the so-called best practices of the hard approach to management. As we will see, these misconceptions don't increase reciprocity; instead, they destroy it:

- *The more clarity, the better.* The first misconception is that an individual's roles and objectives should be as detailed and well defined as possible. Although we certainly don't advocate *confusion* in role-and-responsibility definitions, we believe that a certain degree of *fuzziness* in these definitions can be a good thing. Think back to the relay race. To be sure, it is necessary to clearly define the order of the four sprinters and the specialized roles of, say, the first sprinter, who needs to know how to get out of the blocks quickly. But some aspects of the sprinters' roles cannot and should not be defined precisely in some important gray areas. For instance, at exactly what distance should the sprinter pass the baton to the next—at ninety-six meters? At ninety-seven? When you define roles with too much clarity, it often has the opposite of the desired effect because it allows people to avoid recognizing their interdependencies. Instead, they just adhere to the specification ("I handed it off at ninety-six meters, just as you said.") and check the box next to that responsibility, rather than working with others to find ways to deliver the desired output (a smooth and rapid handoff of the baton) in a given situation. (See the sidebar "Beware Too Much Clarity.")

- *Cooperation dilutes personal responsibility.* The second misconception is that responsibility is always, and can only be, lodged in the individual. "If everyone is responsible, nobody is responsible." But, as we will see, the reality of interdependency is that it is impossible to parse responsibility such that each person's "amount" is perfectly defined. It is also possible to hold more than one person responsible for the same task. In the relay race, for example, two sprinters know they both have responsibility during the twenty meters or so within which the handoff of the baton must take place. If the baton drops in this gray area of the handoff between two runners, both are at fault.

- *Interdependency destroys accountability.* We often hear managers say things like, "How can I be held responsible for results that depend on the performance of others?" The third misconception is that we can be accountable for our work only if we are the sole authority over it and control all the resources necessary to accomplish the task. But it is possible for a person to be accountable without having exclusive control over the resources needed to deliver, as long as others who partly control those resources cooperate.

How do these misconceptions play out in real work situations? No doubt, you have heard employees say, "Boss, please tell me exactly where my responsibility starts and ends in this process.

SIMPLE RULES TOOLKIT

Beware of Too Much Clarity

- Resist the pressure to clarify roles, decision rights, and processes. Try to keep appropriate fuzziness and overlaps between roles.

- Beyond a certain threshold, clarity only encourages mechanistic compliance and "checking the box" behaviors, as opposed to the engagement and initiative to make things work.

The ambiguity is killing us. Nobody knows where his job ends and another person's begins." When somebody asks for clarity in this way, it is frequently an attempt to avoid having to cooperate. If you respond to such a request by offering complete clarity on where the responsibility starts and ends, another question is sure to follow: "OK, well if that's how it is, and I'm going to be held accountable, I'm going to need a few things: equipment, team, budget, and decision rights that clearly match the scope of my responsibility." If you agree, and even if you are careful not to give too many resources, you will discover that you have achieved a "miracle." All the dependencies will disappear and the need for cooperation that goes with them; now the person who asked for clarity has complete self-sufficiency. The individual who is clearly accountable—thanks to that clarified list of responsibilities—can do without others and escape the servitude of cooperation. Each person can tend his or her own garden, not being dependent on others. But at what cost for the company as a

The Difference between Autonomy and Self-Sufficiency

- Autonomy is about fully mobilizing our intelligence and energy to influence outcomes, including those outcomes that we do not entirely control.

- Self-sufficiency is about limiting our efforts only to those outcomes that we control completely without having to depend on others.

- Autonomy is essential for coping with complexity; self-sufficiency is an obstacle because it hinders the cooperation needed to make autonomy effective.

whole? Self-sufficiency may be comfortable, but this kind of comfort is a poor predictor of organizational success. (See the sidebar "The Difference between Autonomy and Self-Sufficiency.")

Industronal: The Challenge of Cutting Costs While Maintaining Quality

In order to address its quality problem, Industronal's management decided to increase the company's investment in research and development. Doing so, however, meant cutting costs in other departments in order to free up the necessary funds for investment. The purchasing departments' contribution to this effort, as senior management defined it, was to cut total purchasing costs by 20 percent, with no erosion in the quality of supplies or in on-time delivery.

The purchasing organization consisted of two quite different roles: the "category strategists" and the "buying units." The role of the category strategist was to develop a strategy for how to buy goods in a particular category, such as raw materials, manufacturing equipment, IT systems, or office furniture. The strategy had to be clear, with detailed specifications pertaining to vendor selection, negotiation, and legal agreements. Once the strategy was set, the category strategists would then create guidelines and develop tools that were used by the buying units. These units were organized by region and handled the orders they received from their internal customers for resources in all categories. The managers of the buying units were expected to follow the category guidelines and deploy the tools to determine how the orders should be processed.

Two Views of the Purchasing Role

The category strategists did their best to come up with innovative ways to cut costs. But they argued that the buying units failed to implement the strategies properly. The buying units, in turn, complained that the strategies weren't practical, that the tools and guidelines were difficult to use, and that applying them took too long. "The category strategists are just a bunch of technocrats," the buying units said. "All they care about is their strategies, their guidelines, and their tools. They don't seem to care what we really need to do our work."

As for the purchasing department's internal customers at Industronal, we observed that they often bypassed the buyers altogether and dealt directly with suppliers of their choice. They generally purchased smaller quantities than the purchasing department did and did not haggle much over prices and terms, but they got what they wanted when they wanted it. To them, the purchasing department had become a constraint, and suppliers were the resource. This direct dealing undercut the relationships the buying units had with the suppliers and made it impossible for them to achieve the targeted cost reduction.

Setting Rich Objectives: Framing Roles for Overall Results

Soon after we got involved with Industronal, we realized that a key part of the solution to the problem was to develop rich objectives for both the category strategists and the buying units. When roles are defined with rich objectives, people at the front line of the organization can make the everyday trade-offs that arise when dealing with multiple performance requirements. With rich objectives, there is less need to put procedures in place to arbitrate conflicts between requirements (or the groups responsible for them) and decisions are less likely to escalate through the organization. (See the sidebar "Rich Objectives.")

Collective Output Objectives

Collective output objectives are those that depend on the involvement of multiple individuals and units. These objectives define the ultimate value the groups involved want to deliver, as defined by external or internal customers, or by other stakeholders. This

KEEP IN MIND

Rich Objectives

Rich objectives stimulate the mutual interest to cooperate by making each person's success depend on the success of others. They have three components:

- *Collective output objectives* define the ultimate value the organization wants to deliver; their achievement depends on the interactions of multiple individuals and work units.

- *Individual input objectives* define the inputs that individuals contribute to the collective output; their achievement does not depend on interactions with other individuals or work groups.

- *Overlap objectives* define what a person does, in his or her role and area, and that increases the effectiveness of others in their own roles and areas.

output is measurable. For the sprinters in the relay race, for example, the collective output objective is to win the race. Winning requires dealing with the complexity of two contradictory requirements: speed and reliability (in passing the baton).

At a high level, output objectives can be formulated in terms of earnings, return on investment, share price (such as at Inter-Lodge), time to market (such as at MobiliTele), or market share (such as at GrandeMart). At a more granular level, output objectives can involve: working capital, gross margin, cost of goods sold, profitability by product, or new-product sales. At Industronal, the collective output objectives defined for the category strategists and the buying units were to reduce the total cost of purchases by 20 percent and to satisfy the needs of internal customers.

Individual Input Objectives

This second component of rich objectives is a contribution or input to the collective output that an individual or discrete unit can make without the significant involvement of other individuals or units. Some aspects of an input objective are measurable, such as the efficiency with which an individual can learn a skill and his or her efficiency in applying that skill.

It takes initiative for individuals to add value to a collective effort. They have to interpret the formal procedures, figure out how to act in the spirit of guidelines, and go beyond the letter of the law. They have to take the specifics of each situation into account, rather than just mechanistically checking off the boxes on the list of procedural steps or action items. There is always a distance—a gap—between real situations and what is defined by procedures. The gap can only be bridged by people using their judgment to best apply procedures. Bridging that gap is how people add value. The greater the complexity of multiple and contradictory performance requirements, the greater the distance between situations and what the rules can instruct.

The individual's efforts are essential to bridge the gap between the design of roles and responsibilities as defined on paper and the real situations in which the tasks must be performed. In the relay race, some input objectives are unique to a specific sprinter—for example, the one who starts the race needs to know how to get out of the blocks quickly. Other input objectives are common to all the sprinters, for instance, each one has to train so that she runs her leg of the race as fast as she possibly can.

At Industronal, the input objective defined for the category strategists was to develop innovative buying strategies. For the managers of the buying units, the input objective was to develop the skills of the members of their buying team. Both kinds of contribution could be objectively assessed to some extent: there are standard optimization levers for procurement strategies that can be used to evaluate their innovativeness, and it is also possible to assess the mastery of new skills. (See the sidebar "Defining Input Objectives.")

Overlap Objectives

Overlap objectives are contributions that only make a positive difference in the performance of others. It is a way to perform tasks that increases the contribution of others to the output. The overlap objective for one sprinter is to transfer the baton in the most effective way for the next sprinter. For this sprinter, the overlap objective is to take the baton in the way that is most effective for the previous runner.

At Industronal, the overlap objective defined for category strategists was to ensure that the guidelines and tools they developed for the buying units were practical and easy to apply. If they considered the gray area intelligently, they could increase the contribution of the buyers to the overall result. For the buyers, the overlap objective was to take into account the category strategies when processing and executing orders. In doing so, they could provide category strategists with more opportunities to go further in developing innovative strategies, instead of having to constantly modify the same ones because they were not applied.

SIMPLE RULES TOOLKIT

Defining Input Objectives

In defining input objectives, make sure the scope of roles is valuable for the individual as well as for the organization. Doing so creates a strong social contract between the company and its people. To accomplish this, ask these two questions:

1. *Will this role and its objectives create a significant learning effect?* Will the effective execution of the role bring about productivity improvements whose benefits can be shared between the company and its employees? Does the role involve individual capabilities that the individuals can enhance as they gain experience in the role?

2. *Is the learning effect sustainable over time?* Will the role become obsolete quickly or will it remain relevant as technology progresses and market trends shift? Input objectives are sustainable when they lead to continuous improvement and education. By making learning a valuable investment for individuals—beyond its value to their current work with the company—you provide a reason for people to engage more fully in their role today.

When you set up overlap objectives, remember that success in overlap objectives is essential for performance (it is indeed the ultimate success factor at the world-class level, for instance, with very strong individual sprinters). But this success—or failure—inherently takes place off the radar screen of objective measurable criteria. The transfer of the baton is a blind spot for metrics: it happens in a gray area where individual contributions cannot be measured. If the baton falls or slows down during the transfer, was it the sprinter who passed the baton or the one who took it who caused the failure? No metric will give you the answer. At Industronal, was the failure to achieve the desired cost reduction of a particular transaction because of the inadequacy of the strategy or of the execution? Similarly, consider the extent to which the category strategists pay attention to the practical applicability of the guidelines and tools they develop for the buying units. There are no objective measurable criteria in these gray areas. Only when the buyers try to put a guideline or tool to use can they feel if it is practical or not. When they use a tool well, is it because it is very practical, thanks to the category strategists' efforts or because of the diligence of the buyers? Measurement cannot disentangle contributions to overlap objectives.[1] What gets measured gets done, yes. But if we only use measurement to reward performance, what gets done is at the expense of what cannot be measured: cooperation. We get a series of accurate metrics that show how well each and every silo is doing, while in fact the company's overall performance may be disastrous.

Three Reinforcing Mechanisms

By defining these rich objectives, we made visible the overall complexity of the performance requirements (quality, quantity, on-time delivery, and cost reduction) and embedded them in everyone's roles and objectives. Complexity was brought to the front line.

Defining rich objectives is an important way to increase reciprocity within an organization. But in the end, such objectives are only an expression of intent. How can you create a work context such that individuals actually behave in accordance with these objectives? There are three reinforcing mechanisms that managers can use to increase the odds that people will behave according to the rich objectives—eliminating internal monopolies, reducing some resources, and creating adequate networks for interactions. We conclude our discussion of increasing reciprocity by considering the positive role these actions can play.

Eliminate Internal Monopolies

Monopolies take many forms. They can be administrations, companies, departments, or individuals. They may be upstream units that affect what can be done by downstream units or a specialist or expert role, such as a legal department.

Monopolies cannot be avoided by others in the organization. Other units have no alternative but to work with the monopoly, so the units that depend on the cooperation of monopolies are stuck. Given that other units are fully dependent on them, monopolies do not take into account the needs and constraints of those units. Because they have total control of their own resources, monopolies can work around their own constraints.

This is why monopolies, whatever form they take, become bureaucratic. They stress the importance of rules and create many of their own. Rules add legitimacy to the internal constraints the monopoly forces others to adjust to.[2]

An internal monopoly can, however, be broken, either by making it contestable or by finding a partial substitute for it.

By making it contestable, we mean that no function, by virtue of its organizational decision rights, should be protected from questioning by others about matters such as budgeting, investments, or even career decisions for its staff. If monopolies are immune from challenge over such decisions, they begin to exhibit silo behaviors.

Invoking the dictum "the right person in the right place" is a very effective way for internal monopolies to ward off challenges. If an outsider questions the results, actions, or decisions of someone inside the monopoly, it is interpreted as a personal attack and a threat to efficiency. Monopolies, whether individuals or units, typically counter such attacks by claiming possession of special knowledge or expertise that the attacker does not possess and cannot possibly understand (the transceiver engineers at MobiliTele used to claim that the other units could never understand the complex evolution of the international standards for transceiver technology). But even if members of a function do possess expertise or knowledge that is relatively rare in the organization, that should not preclude others from having a say in the matter, whatever it might be.

At the consumer goods company L'Oréal, for example, during its period of extremely rapid organic growth, every decision relating to the development and launch of new products was made by a team whose members represented R&D, manufacturing, sales, and communications. At the time, there was no dedicated marketing function. Management had decided that no function could or should have a monopoly on customer knowledge, customer insight, and customer-related decisions; no one function would be allowed to speak exclusively for the customer. Decisions about what products to develop and how and when to launch them were made through a confrontation of ideas brought forward and supported by the different participants. These decisions were made in what was sometimes called "the confrontation room." In that room, everything and everyone could be contested, which is an efficient and effective way to push along the decision process and to get better decisions.

In addition to making every group contestable, you can also break a monopoly by making it partly substitutable. To do this, you make sure there is some form of substitution available that provides an alternative to the monopoly and therefore keeps the people in the monopoly on their toes. The substitute may be available from other internal roles or from an outside source.

Eliminating an internal monopoly at a robotics manufacturer. A manufacturer of robotics had a problem. The company was always late in launching innovations, among the last among its competitors to integrate new technologies into its products. What's more, its costs were out of line with industry norms. Management explained the problem as one of psychology: "Our company is not innovative enough because our research and development engineers are not creative enough." The solution was to require the engineers to attend creativity workshops. The initiative only made things worse.

When we analyzed the work context, we realized that the real goal of the hardware and software units was to be recognized as the creator of a new innovation. After all, the responsible unit would often have a larger budget and more autonomy as a result. When hardware and software cooperated, however, it was difficult for the head of R&D to know which unit was really responsible for the subsequent innovation. Each unit's behavior was therefore to work in isolation, as long as it took to guarantee that any innovation could be traced back unequivocally to its origin: "We are often the real creator of the new thing, but management doesn't know it if the hardware and software teams bring their elements together too early in the process."

The creativity workshop had only allowed each unit to work longer and deeper (and, one hopes, more creatively) in isolation from the others. Given this tendency, it was not surprising that when the hardware and software were eventually put together, nine times out of ten they were incompatible. Numerous modifications were necessary to make the overall product work, further adding to cost and delays.

Improving creativity is a great lever to use, but, as with any interventions, you must first understand why people do what they do. It is not the lever that matters, but how it will shape the work context, what impact it has on the goals, resources, and constraints. An important resource of the robotics company's hardware and software units was that they were internal monopolies and could therefore make the rest of the organization bear the consequence of their lack of cooperation. So they became creative monopolies, at the greater expense of the organization.

To create a substitute for these units, we recommended that the marketing department start forming alliances with external research centers. By giving people in marketing a choice of who they could work with (they could now control a stake for R&D), the company was able to ensure better cooperation from the internal R&D units. A marginal opening of the organization to external sources of knowledge and expertise was sufficient and far more effective than forcing the use of scorecards, KPIs, controls, and incentives. Within two years, the company surpassed its best competitors in speed of releasing successful innovations and at a comparable cost.

Reduce Some Resources

The second mechanism to reinforce rich objectives to increase reciprocity is to reduce resources. You might assume that, in order to reduce resources, you first have to improve cooperation, which frees up resources so they can then be cut back. This is true, but you can also do it the other way around: make a reduction in resources to impel cooperation. At home, you will have much more luck creating cooperation by removing the extra TVs than by first requiring everyone to read up on game theory.

At Industronal, the management team decided to cut the purchasing budget of the internal customers and, at the same time, set rich objectives for the two units of the purchasing organization. With fewer resources available, the internal customers had no choice but to cooperate with the purchasing units. In this way, purchasing shifted from being a constraint to being a resource for internal users.

When resources are plentiful, each person or group can act alone. These resources are not used to create value, but just to allow dysfunctional self-sufficiency and often to create monopolies. The abundance of resources basically removes interdependencies and the need to cooperate. A unit can use excess resources to provide a buffer that ensures it is not affected by what happens in other functions. If there is plenty of extra inventory on hand, for example, that reduces the need for procurement and manufacturing to cooperate. The problem of extra resources, in many cases, is not their cost but that they allow people to avoid real cooperation.

When resources are removed, people have to share. They become more interdependent, more affected by what happens to others, and therefore more likely to take into account the effect on others of what they do. Putting others in a bad situation may backfire because people are likely to be reciprocally affected. The feedback loop is based on interaction between what happens to each one. You can then avoid the bureaucracy of internal contracts, service level agreements, and so on.

One of the most important resources in any organization is time. If people have the time they need according to their own procedures, they don't need to account for the situation and needs of others. At MobiliTele, the manufacturer of telecoms systems, delays—an overconsumption of the time resource—created a bubble within which each of the engineering units could work independently of the others.

The reverse is also true: if people don't have enough time to complete their tasks according to their own resources, they lose the comfort of having to attend only to their own devices. This is why organizations, when confronted with the urgency of a crisis, will experience a much higher level of cooperation than normal.

In a crisis, people are acutely aware of the need for reciprocity. Everyone is affected. If I don't help you, we will go down together.

The goal of reducing resources is to enhance capabilities, not cut costs. There is a major difference between reducing resources with the explicit purpose of increasing reciprocity and reducing resources simply to cut costs. The former takes into account the complex dynamics that surround cooperation. The latter typically does not.

An organization always needs to consume more resources to compensate for deficient cooperation: time (delays), equipment, systems, teams, working capital in the form of stock when procurement and manufacturing do not cooperate, and so on. So who pays the cost of this overconsumption of resources? In today's complex business environment, both customers and shareholders have more and more options. They will eventually refuse to bear the cost of the extra resources. Who is left to bear the cost? The organization's employees. They must provide more and more individual efforts. But working harder (and sometimes longer) never fully compensates for the lack of cooperation. All too often the only result is increased disengagement or burnout.[3]

When cost cutting is done without understanding the opportunities for superior performance through cooperation, an organization may improve short-term productivity, but at the cost of diminishing its capabilities. Sometimes, those capabilities become so degraded that they result in product defects, mistakes, safety problems, and missed strategic opportunities. By contrast, when an organization cuts resources as part of a plan to impel people to cooperate, the result is superior group capability. Not only do costs fall; innovation and product quality can also improve.

Lack of cooperation not only has a negative effect on the company's ability to satisfy multiple performance requirements; it also can erode the productivity improvements the company may have realized through other means, such as technological innovations, scale, and the experience effect. The use of information and communications technologies (ICTs) in conjunction with modern management methods may produce something that *looks* like a productivity gain, in the form of reduced waiting periods or shorter downtimes. That is, there are more minutes of work achieved per hour of employee presence in the workplace. But, without cooperation, the value produced in those extra minutes actually decreases because of the proliferation of non-value-adding activities (rework, modifications, writing reports, control, and so on). Without the conditions to get cooperation, ICTs not only do not realize their full potential, they can also be used to avoid real cooperation—think about the multiple cc's in e-mails and the meeting requests sent to ten or more invitees to a conference call. Is this real cooperation or a way to protect ourselves?

Multiplexity: Create Networks of Interaction

A third way to reinforce the rich objectives that increase reciprocity is to make sure people belong to multiple networks of interactions that complement each other. This is what we call "multiplexity." In addition to designing rich objectives for the purchasing unit and removing some resources from the purchasing budgets of the line organization, Industronal management also created three interaction networks in order to put people in situations where they felt compelled to confront their multiple performance requirements. This was particularly important to ensure an effective contribution in the gray area where no objective measurable criteria, let alone incentive, could be used. In any case, given the financial situation of the company, it could not rely on incentives, whether the objectives were measurable or not.

The first network consisted of the category strategists, the managers of the buying units, and their internal customers. Every two weeks, these three groups met to review progress in filling orders. The internal customers could voice their concerns: "When are my supplies arriving? Will my order be on spec, or will I get a shock when I see it?" If internal customers thought there was a problem with the category strategy, they could complain to the strategists. They had little interest in how innovative the category strategy was. If it did not help the buyer deliver the goods to the required specifications for quality, quantity, and delivery time, it was of no value to them.

The second network of interactions consisted entirely of the category strategists and took the form of what is often called a "community of practice."[4] They periodically got together, and each category leader presented his or her latest buying strategy to the rest of the group. Unlike in the progress review with the internal customers who didn't care much about innovation, the innovativeness of the strategy mattered a great deal in these meetings. The strategists were keen to hear about and evaluate their peers on the degree of insight and creativity in the strategy. How did it exploit (or ignore) specific procurement optimization levers such as bundling, supplier management, demand management, order standardization, and in-sourcing opportunities? As one participant put it, "It is like a TED talk for category strategists." If a strategist performed poorly, he or she would lose face and reputation.

The third network was another community of practice, this time for the managers of the buying units. They would get together to compare the productivity of their teams and how fast they were learning new skills.

In all three networks, the people involved were focusing on the same pieces of work: the specific purchasing requests, with the corresponding category strategy; the guidelines and tools; the savings targets; the order specifications; and deadlines. But each network examined the results from a different perspective. Together, the three perspectives captured all the performance requirements, even when they were contradictory. This was not achieved through conflicting orders from above but through flexible interactions. In these interaction networks, people were exposed to significant risks, such as feeling the wrath of their frustrated internal customers or suffering the loss of reputation with peers. In such feedback loops, the stake of saving face is very high.[5] Symmetrically, the satisfaction of successfully performing in these interaction networks was also very high. This kind of satisfaction is generally very rare in purchasing units. At best, when things go well, purchasing is transparent for others, and people don't feel pride for being transparent.

Each individual—category strategist or buying manager—was part of more than one network of interactions. Each network dealt with a subset of performance requirements and also contained a feedback loop. Belonging to multiple networks—multiplexity—impelled the individuals to contribute in his or her specialized role to the multiple performance areas: innovativeness, practicality, buyer productivity, and the satisfaction of customer needs. By being at the intersection of the various networks of interactions, the individual eventually had to satisfy the union of the requirements in play.

Because of the rich objectives and reinforcing mechanisms, the purchasing organization at Industronal ultimately met its

20 percent cost-reduction target. It also received the highest possible rating on satisfaction from its internal customers.

Multiplexity is a way to avoid the hard fixes of procedures, scorecards, and control mechanisms, including all the documentation and monitoring they require. The feedback loops within the networks impel people to fully apply their intelligence and knowledge while benefiting from the cooperation of others.

Greater Accountability, Less Complicatedness

Increasing reciprocity addresses the question of accountability, which becomes more and more critical as the need to satisfy multiple performance requirements puts organizations in situations where they need to achieve both differentiation (that is, specialization for greater expertise or for more local responsiveness) and also greater integration (fluid and end-to-end cross-functional efficiency). They can do so by framing rich objectives and then embedding feedback loops that retain the benefits of specialization while ensuring a synergistic interplay. The effect is that capabilities are more distributed throughout the organization. It is much like the brain, where functions such as language do not emerge from one physical area of the brain, but from the interactions across many different areas.

Simple rule four also helps managers push back against the intense pressure to clarify responsibilities and situations, a pressure that tends to be counterproductive. It helps them understand—from a performance and organizational point of view—where clarity is needed and adds value as opposed to where it is superfluous or even detrimental to performance.

There is also a direct effect on complicatedness. By setting overlap objectives, you can avoid the creation of middle offices. In the relay race, there is no coordinating sprinter whose role is to take the baton from one sprinter and give it to the next. The feedback loops created by eliminating internal monopolies, removing some resources, and creating multiplexity allow you to avoid the need for multiple scorecards, compliance metrics, and incentives. These feedback loops allow for decentralized control, since it is based on interaction among people, each one partly controlling the behavior of others. Control becomes distributed and flexible, as opposed to top down and rigid, which enables the organization to be more adaptive to changing conditions.

SUMMARY OF SIMPLE RULE FOUR

In the face of business complexity, work is becoming more interdependent. To meet multiple and often contradictory performance requirements, people need to rely more on each other. They need to cooperate directly instead of relying on dedicated interfaces, coordination structures or procedures that only add to complicatedness. *Reciprocity* is the recognition by people or units in an organization that they have a *mutual interest* in cooperation and that the success of one depends on the success of others (and vice versa). The way to create that reciprocity is by setting *rich objectives* and reinforcing them by eliminating monopolies, reducing resources, and creating new networks of interaction.

5

Simple Rule Five

Extend the Shadow of the Future

I n this chapter, we will describe a rule that creates feedback loops in a very particular and powerful way by exploiting the effect of *time*. What game theory calls the "shadow of the future" is the importance of what happens tomorrow to us as a result of what we do today. By extending the shadow of the future, we make the more-or-less distant horizon—that point at which our present behavior will eventually reveal its consequences—much more important and evident to us now. To extend the shadow of the future you need to create feedback loops that make people feel the consequences of how they deal with multiple performance requirements sooner, more frequently, and for longer periods of time.

In this chapter, you will learn:

- **How to recognize the traps of strategic alignment.** One of the major reasons that people often remain unconnected from the consequences of their actions is their organization's adherence to the idea of *strategic alignment*. Strategic alignment is a sophisticated form of the hard approach that is extremely popular today. As you might expect, however, the standard practice of strategic alignment only adds to organizational complicatedness, blocks cooperation, and has a deleterious effect on overall performance.

- **How to use feedback loops based on time to create a more effective work context.** We will offer four different ways for extending the shadow of the future: tightening the feedback loop by increasing the frequency of interactions, bringing the end point forward, tying futures together, and making people walk in the shoes they make for others. This simple rule draws the most heavily on game theory and Axelrod's thinking on the evolution of cooperation. However, our work in organizational analysis and experience with executive teams has sometimes led us to recommendations that might seem to contradict Axelrod. But, as you will see, at a deeper level, there is no contradiction.

We will illustrate the perils of strategic alignment and the benefits of extending the shadow of the future using a variety of case studies. We will pay special attention to the story of MotorFleet, a manufacturer that was struggling to incorporate a new performance requirement—the reparability of its vehicles—among the many requirements (cost, quality, safety, energy consumption, time-to-market, and so on) that it already had.

Strategic Alignment: A Trap of Complicatedness

What do managers mean by strategic alignment? If it means the organization must be designed to support rather than hinder the execution of the strategy, then it's simply a truism and not very helpful. Who would argue that structures, processes, and systems should not help in the execution of strategy?

In fact, what managers mean when they use this term is often far more specific and elaborate than a simple truism, and this is where the problem starts. The standard practice of strategic alignment has three major limitations:

- It takes a mechanistic approach that, when confronted with the realities of business complexity, turns the organization into the equivalent of a "stupid machine."

- It binds the organization to a linear design sequence that only ties people up into knots.

- It creates bad organizations that can only develop bad strategies.

A Stupid Machine

In its crudest form, strategic alignment is the mechanistic application of the well-known mantra: "from strategy to structure."[1] To understand the problem with this approach, imagine that an organization is a stupid machine that has but one routine: each time a new performance requirement is introduced, the machine adds a new, dedicated function to handle it: "Quality is a new requirement. Add one quality department to the organizational machine."

As we have seen, the number of performance requirements has grown roughly sixfold over the past fifty-five years, which means that our stupid machine would have had to gear each new dedicated function with all the existing ones, such that complicatedness would multiply by at least thirty-six times.[2] This is distressingly close to the increase in our complicatedness index (described in the introduction): thirty-five times. In other words, the corporate world has actually evolved almost exactly as our imaginary organization machine has: asymptotically to maximum mechanistic stupidity.

A Linear Sequence That Ties Us into Knots

Often when companies follow the "from strategy to structure" mantra, they use a linear sequence. They start with strategy, then align the structures, then align processes within the structures, and then align various systems (IT, performance monitoring, human resource management, and so on) to make the processes work. At each step of the sequence, however, it becomes increasingly difficult to address the right issues or to provide useful answers.

For example, once you create a middle office—between the back office, which is dedicated to standardization, and the front office, which is dedicated to customization—the next step in the sequence is to align the systems to the structure you have created. So you ask the IT department to design management information systems for the managers in the middle office, and you give the HR department the task of providing recruitment, training, incentives, and career paths for all the middle-office employees. Functions such as IT and HR are under pressure to create value and behave like "business partners," so they do what they can to deliver. They are not allowed to ask the most important questions, however: "Why do we need a middle office in the first place? Can't we get the front and back offices to cooperate and have *them* reconcile the issues of standardization and customization?"

In such situations, the talent and expertise of IT and HR managers will only be applied to make the wrong solution even more sophisticated. The HR function, for example, is best positioned to see the ways that complicated mechanisms cause suffering at work and help develop solutions, but it is forced into aiding and abetting the old obsolete approaches. HR managers scurry around trying to find ways to improve the leadership style of the disengaged middle-office manager (but how can he or she get engaged, given that he or she is powerless in the role and just an interface?). The same is true of other functions and systems. The strategic alignment sequence prevents companies from fully leveraging the real potential of information technologies.[3]

Bad Organization Drives Bad Strategy

Yes, the organization must be in the service of the strategy, but it is also true that the organization—because of its design and way of working—determines the very content of strategic choices, not only their execution. This is why the line that separates strategy from organization has become increasingly blurry, especially as competitive advantage derives more and more from agility, flexibility, and adaptiveness. Indeed, all these capabilities are rooted in the combination of autonomy and cooperation that we described at the beginning of the book.

The problem is that the kind of complicated organization that results from strategic alignment always comes up with bad strategies.[4] This is because a complicated organization cannot help but have a fragmented view of its competitive landscape. The information it gathers about customers, suppliers, competitors, and regulators remains scattered across functions, business lines, and geographies. The organization is unable to accumulate and link these various inputs into a holistic understanding of the opportunities and threats the strategy needs to address. At the robotics company we discussed in chapter 4, for example, because the R&D units did not cooperate, they were unable to connect the dots and thus could not detect the real opportunities for innovation in their markets.

In some cases, the bad strategy will drive the overcomplicated company to take on new performance requirements—such as a wider product portfolio or more service features—that it is not prepared to handle. Almost without fail, it will produce the new products at extra cost or with high levels of defects, or be unable to deliver them on time. Then, to stay competitive and retain customers, the company will be forced to take remedial steps, such as lowering prices or adding product features.

When this happens, the company eventually becomes unable to distinguish between the performance requirements that really could create value (such as a wider product selection) and the actions that have been taken as concessions to customers, suppliers, or distributors (such as piling on extra features) because of the declining bargaining power that results from poor performance. The less effective the company is in addressing business complexity, the more complexity it ends up having to assimilate, with declining results. It not only does things wrong, it does the wrong things. Beyond inflating the quantity of input, complicatedness deflates the quality of outputs.

Examples abound. A high-tech manufacturer we know hired three thousand people (20 percent of its workforce) over a four-year period. Two thousand of them went into coordination or interface roles. One result was that the company, which had about twenty-five customers, made about thirty different products. This amount of customization was not required to be competitive in this market. When the company removed all the coordination and interface roles, and instead made marketing, R&D, and sales

SIMPLE RULES TOOLKIT

Avoid the Trap of Strategic Alignment

When a new performance requirement emerges, do not follow the traditional sequence: from strategy to structures, to processes, to systems, to metrics, to incentives, to career paths. If you do, you will only add many complicating elements and are bound to miss the smart simplicity solution. Instead, link the new requirement to what people do today using feedback loops. Using simple rule five, you can ensure that the results you want to see in the future are already embedded in people's choice of action today.

people act as integrators, their cooperation allowed it to detect commonalities across customer needs and to better standardize systems, platforms, and components. Market share and profitability grew. (See the sidebar "Avoid the Trap of Strategic Alignment.")

Four Ways to Extend the Shadow of the Future

How can you avoid following the path of strategic alignment but still ensure that the organization produces good strategies and implements them well? By using the simple rules and, in particular, simple rule five. There are four ways to extend the shadow of the future: tightening the feedback loop by increasing the frequency of interactions, bringing the end point forward, tying futures together, and making people walk in the shoes they make for others.

Tighten the Feedback Loops

One way is to tighten feedback loops by having people interact more frequently with others whose work is affected by their actions. Ideally, these interactions should be direct encounters that make it impossible for people to ignore facts about how well they have dealt with the multiple requirements of performance.

For example, you can increase the frequency with which your people review collective results. At the robotics company with the innovation problem ("Our engineers aren't creative enough"), in addition to removing internal monopolies, management also decided that the company should hold progress reviews, not once every six months, the practice in the past, but once every two weeks. This change had an immediate and dramatic impact on the two engineering groups. When the review was conducted at six-month intervals, the engineers could avoid delivering on their commitments, could fail to cooperate, and could ignore their colleagues for as long as five months and twenty-nine days. Now, the engineers could avoid facing the consequences of their actions for only thirteen days.

Lack of cooperation backfires faster when the feedback loop is tighter. The net present value of doing well increases for the individual because the future consequences—the pain of facing a difficult moment when your failure to stick to your commitment becomes obvious—are discounted over a shorter period. At the robotics company, cooperation between the hardware and software engineers immediately increased, and so, therefore, did innovativeness.

Bring the End Point Forward

The shadow of the future can be extended by making sure people's involvement in the work continues to the end point of the activity—the point at which the consequences of their actions show up in collective results. This can be achieved by bringing the end point forward in time or by making sure people cannot leave their role until they reach the end point and experience the consequences of their actions themselves.

One way to bring the end point forward is to shorten the duration of a project. Suppose that a company embarks on a *three-year* project. If you are involved, you can be fairly sure you will no longer be around when it is completed. You will have moved to another job or location within the company, been promoted out of operations, retired, or gone to a different company. As a result, you can be reasonably sure you won't be directly affected by the consequences of the actions you take now or how well you cooperate during the time you are involved.

If, instead, the company launches a project designed to deliver meaningful results—with clear milestones, reviews, and deliverables—within *nine* months, your sense of the future is dramatically altered. Now, as a member of the original project team, you are no longer so sure that you'll be out of the picture when the project delivers its results, if it does deliver. You have little choice but to assume you *will* be exposed to the outcomes and to act accordingly.

Axelrod advocates an increase in *duration* (the period during which interactions take place and people bear the consequences of their cooperation or lack thereof) as a way to enhance cooperation. On the contrary, we advocate shorter timelines. However, there is no contradiction if you bear in mind the real issue. By shortening the objective duration of a project, you extend the subjective duration for the individual: "I am in this from the beginning to the end."

Tie Futures Together

A third way to extend the shadow of the future is by tying futures together. A mining company, operating in developing economies, did this to deal with an issue very common to these countries—the competition for talent.

The mining company had to satisfy seven major performance requirements in order to gain competitive advantage. These requirements related to revenues, discoveries and reserves, safety, cost, operational excellence, sustainability, and working capital optimization. The requirements were further broken down into KPIs customized for each major function and job level. For instance, the site managers—those directly in charge of looking after the mines—had a scorecard with fifteen metrics and related incentives, all of which pertained to the seven performance requirements. Those dispatching mined material, for example, had indicators on productivity and service levels designed to ensure operational excellence. Each metric was weighted to line up behaviors with the relative importance of the performance requirements.

It became very important for the company to develop its next generation of site managers, because there were not enough qualified and experienced candidates in the local job market to fill the site manager positions. The company decided, therefore, it would have to develop talent internally rather than recruit managers from the outside.

You can guess what happened next. Following the strategic alignment sequence, the central HR department added a new KPI to the site manager's scorecard: talent development. This KPI was broken down into four sub-metrics:

- The spread in the marks the site managers gave to their direct reports, which had to comply with a forced ranking.

- The upward feedback they were receiving from their subordinates.

- The number of training events they were facilitating.

- The new skills acquired by their reports as the result of on-the-job learning.

Rules, metrics, and processes! As it turned out, none of these had any positive impact and site managers continued to do a poor job of developing talent. The main reason was that these solutions missed the central issue of complexity; they did not help reconcile the contradictory requirements of productivity and learning.

Here's why. To achieve any results on the productivity requirement, the site managers knew it was best to assign people to tasks they were familiar with and could perform effectively, even though they wouldn't gain new knowledge or further develop their skills. To succeed on the learning requirement, however, the site managers had to conduct on-the-job training, which required them to assign people to unfamiliar tasks they needed to learn. This had a negative effect on productivity. No wonder the site managers almost always opted for short-term productivity—which is easier to effect and to measure—at the expense of longer-term development of their teams.

Seeing that the competition for talent could not be won through the addition of new metrics, the mining company took a different tack. It found a way to make the site managers directly experience the consequence of not developing the next generation of managers: the company announced that a manager would be promoted only if he or she could propose at least two qualified candidates to take over the job.

This new criterion for promotion embedded a feedback loop that exposed the site managers to the consequences of the trade-off they achieved in reconciling productivity and talent development. The future for a manager was tied to that of his or her replacement, and the futures of both were tied to performance requirements that were contradictory in the short-term.

The feedback loop impelled the site managers to think and behave differently because the shadow of the future had been cast upon them. They realized they had to alter what they had to do to achieve productivity and to develop staff. They began to staff some projects with less experienced subordinates, even when more productive colleagues were available, so the former would have more opportunities to learn and improve their skills.

This was not as easy as it might sound. Each project has its specific constraints (such as risks, urgencies, and challenges), and each subordinate has his or her own characteristics (areas for improvement, experience, and strengths). The site manager had to take all these elements into account and make the best decision for each situation. There were some projects in which a subordinate could take on new tasks without the risk of putting a huge dent in productivity. There were other projects, however, where productivity was the paramount concern and on-the-job learning had to take a backseat. Nobody was better positioned than the site managers to assess the unique circumstances in the here and now of each situation. The new feedback loop impelled them to use all this information and their judgment to come to superior solutions in reconciling the requirements of talent development with short-term productivity. These solutions could not be attained in the previous arrangement, no matter how exhaustive the predefined procedures were or the sophistication of the balanced scorecards and incentives that were meant to align behaviors with the performance requirements.

Make People Walk in the Shoes They Have
Made for Others

The fourth way to extend the shadow of the future is to make people take on the role that others play, if only temporarily. This is particularly effective when there are long time lags between related decisions or when the outcomes of people's decisions will not be evident until so far in the future that they may never encounter those who are affected. By causing people to walk in the shoes they have made for others—that is, people they don't work directly with and might not otherwise meet—they are exposed to the problems their present behaviors could pose for them in the future.

MotorFleet: Making the Engineers Understand the Issue of Reparability

Consider the case of MotorFleet, a vehicle manufacturer that was laboring to meet several performance requirements, including cost, safety, product compactness, energy consumption, and anticorrosion performance.

To meet these requirements, the organization had rigorously applied the strategic alignment sequence. Different functions standardized product platforms to achieve scale economies. Project units customized products to satisfy distinct customer segments. Engineering divisions were organized according to specific requirements defined by marketing and also by technical specialization. There was a rampancy of roles, processes, KPIs, and incentives for each requirement.

Then MotorFleet's key competitor added to the new business complexity that the vehicle manufacturer had to face. The competitor announced it would extend its warranty period to five years, during which major repairs for products that were similar to MotorFleet's would be covered. MotorFleet's standard warranty was just two years. The manufacturer had to respond by matching the five-year warranty or better.

Mr. Reparability Cannot Fix the Problem . . .

To any manufacturer, the cost of a warranty period depends to a large extent on how quickly the product can be serviced or repaired. Suppose, for example, that the engine has to be removed to fix the headlights. The repair could take at least three days, with a disastrous effect on the warranty budget. So MotorFleet's ability to offer a warranty period similar to that of its competition came down to the reparability of its vehicles, which is, of course, determined by its design team.

MotorFleet knew very well that its vehicles were not easy to repair, but no one really knew who was accountable for this phenomenon called reparability. Nobody was. Everybody was. The management team decided something had to be done: "Reparability is of the upmost importance to our ability to compete. We must have accountability!" You see how easy it is to fall into the strategic alignment trap: "Since there is a new requirement, let's create a new function to be in charge of it."

A reparability function was duly established to coordinate all the decisions that affected reparability across all the engineering specialties—notably, the mechanical and electrical groups. Management also defined a reparability process and a set of performance indicators and incentives to go with it. At the top of this unit was a uniquely accountable role that we call Mr. Reparability.

The reparability challenge was particularly difficult for the mechanical and electrical engineers who worked on the smaller vehicles. To create a competitively compact product, design engineers had come up with a housing that left less room than the mechanical engineers would have liked to fit an engine. The mechanical engineers' solution was to encroach just a tiny bit on the space left to the electrical engineers for their wiring and other components. The electrical engineers then had to find a way to squeeze it all in, which they did by placing some of the wiring in hard-to-access areas. This, in turn, meant that their after-sales service colleagues had to perform lengthy and costly repair operations. Some of these compromises could have been avoided with the use of more expensive components, which would have made repair less likely and less necessary, but that would have made the product's cost uncompetitively high.

The contradictions among compactness, low cost, and reparability were not new for MotorFleet. What was new was the competitive pressure that removed the possibility of satisfying one requirement at the expense of the others.

MotorFleet had already created functions like that of Mr. Reparability for other requirements. There was a Ms. Cost, a Ms. Safety, a Mr. Energy Consumption, and several more. Each of these defined its processes, KPIs, and incentives to align engineers with a specific requirement. The idea, typical of strategic alignment, was that if there are as many KPIs as there are requirements, each with the adequate weight and right incentive, the engineers' behaviors will necessarily place themselves at the weighted average of KPIs in the scorecards.

What was the effect of the new reparability function on the engineers? Because of all the other KPIs and incentives, and despite a relatively large proportion of variable compensation (more than fifteen percent in some cases), a good achievement on the reparability KPI could only make a tiny difference in the total compensation per engineer—a miniscule 0.8 percent. In other words, nothing. We know that incentives can actually have a counterproductive effect on behaviors but, in this case, the effect was neither counterproductive nor effective; it was just negligible, with no impact on the reparability of vehicles.[5]

To deal with this mass of processes, procedures, and rules (MotorFleet's handbook eventually ballooned to include some ten thousand operating procedures), the engineers resorted to their informal network of friends and colleagues to find solutions. They counted on good interpersonal relationships to get by. But the limitation of informal networks is that people all do their best to avoid making any tough decisions that could impose adjustment costs on one another and thus jeopardize the good feelings. In the informal network, the resource is good relationships with others. To preserve this key resource, people tend to avoid difficult trade-offs that, were they to address them, would strain their relationships and, thus, damage their key resource. Moreover, the various bonding events that had been organized to bring the mechanical and electrical engineers together had actually worked. They did feel closer kinship and that made them even more reluctant to strain their relationships and effectively cooperate.

When the tough choices had to be made about contradictory requirements, decisions inevitably got booted upstairs where senior engineering managers, with less direct knowledge of the issues, accepted poor compromises. The after-sales teams continued to struggle with costly repair operations, and MotorFleet found it impossible to extend the warranty period without wrecking the budget. The company was unable to add value by reconciling reparability with the other requirements, but spent a great deal of money and added a lot of complicatedness in the attempt.

. . . But Cooperation Can

At last, MotorFleet changed its approach. Instead of framing the issue according to the principles of strategic alignment—"we need reparability, so we need a reparability structure, with reparability processes and systems"—executives realized the issue was cooperation:

- When engineers designed the vehicles, they would have to take into account the constraints of the service people who would repair them.

- Engineers, notably in the mechanical and electrical units, would have to cooperate with one another, given the impact their combined decisions had on the work of the mechanics in the after-sales garages.

This reframing of the issue radically changed the terms of the problem. Instead of making procedures and scorecards more sophisticated by using the best practice of strategic alignment, the management team decided to find a way to make the insufficient cooperation of engineers become a constraint for them.

For years, the cost of their lack of cooperation had been externalized, pushed onto the after-sales network—particularly, the garage mechanics—and customers as well. How could the context be changed to reintroduce this cost as a constraint for the engineers? How could they be exposed to the consequences of their actions on others and the overall results?

The answer was to make engineers walk in the shoes they had made for others, specifically the after-sales mechanics, with an elegant and ingenious solution: some of the engineers were assigned to work in the company's after-sales network of garages after the launch of a model they had designed. Their responsibility was to manage the warranty budget for that particular model. If the warranty budget exploded because of the hard-to-repair design choices they made, it would explode in their hands. The prospect of being asked to work in the after-sales network—the implied time bomb—had a far more powerful effect on the quality the engineers delivered than could any amount of interfaces, coordinators, or formal metrics.

When the mechanical and electrical engineers fully understood that they might have to deal personally with the consequences of their choices, they began to work in a very different way. They abandoned the touchy-feely approach to teamwork, with its convivial avoidance of real cooperation, and started to address head-on the need for tough solutions. By working with marketing and with each other, the engineers were able to make choices that eventually enabled MotorFleet to match its warranty period with that of its competitors without compromising its other performance requirements.

Of course, the solution involved the adjustment of the organization, but just one element—career paths.[6] But if the management team had continued to strive for strategic align-ment, it would have found it impossible to come up with this elegant solution. That's because career paths come too late in the linear sequence of alignment. Senior executives would not have considered career paths until they had aligned everything else—structures, processes, and systems. The responsibility for adjust-ing the career paths would have fallen to an HR person who would only have been asked to make Mr. Reparability's compen-sation, benefits, and career path suitably attractive—thus fur-ther increasing complicatedness.

The new career path for engineers reduced some of the benefits that might have been gained from continued experience within their group (such as the intense learning that comes from repeat-ing a task or the innovation that can result from single-minded focus), but the analysis showed that such potential productiv-ity improvements were insignificant compared to the benefits of greater cooperation between engineers and with the after-sales network.

As simple rule five was implemented, the management team found that it opened up opportunities to apply some of the other simple rules, such as reinforcing the role of integrators. The company was able to remove the cross-functional coordinators (including the reparability structure), interfacing roles, processes, scorecards, and incentives. Eighty percent of those in interface roles were returned to positions where they could cooperate with others in satisfying the multiple requirements of performance. Within three years, overall productivity at MotorFleet increased by 20 percent, and the company now makes its extended war-ranty the cornerstone of its communication campaign.

The Effect of the Extended Shadow: Increased Engagement

Extending the shadow of the future changes what people have at stake—their goals and problems—and often it constrains what they have to do by taking into account the constraints of others, not only their own. This is why, when extending the shadow of the future, people must be granted sufficient autonomy and room to maneuver. It would be absurd (and unjust) to expose people to the consequences of their actions without giving them enough say in how they can act or by preventing them from taking any actions that might have an impact on future results. If an outcome makes a difference for you, you should be able to make a difference in the outcome. Without room of maneuver and enough influence on those whose cooperation people need, a feedback loop only traps them. When that happens, the only way to deal with that kind of suffering is to disengage or, as the receptionists at InterLodge did, resign.

Engagement, therefore, is prospective, not retrospective. People do not choose to engage as a result of gratitude for how things have gone in the past, but rather as a reflection of what it will bring them. By extending the shadow of the future, a company makes people's engagement more worthwhile to them because they have the ability to make a greater difference in their personal trajectory. The potential is all the greater because the trajectory is not fixed and people can help create a better career for themselves where they are, rather than moving to another company or endeavor. To get this kind of engagement, companies have to create plenty of room to maneuver within roles and set up career paths that enable people to grow in various ways, by rising to a higher position or by enriching and broadening their current role as they create more value.

When people do not have any ability to affect the things that matter to them, it can be highly demotivating. This is proving to be especially true for senior populations in the workforce. Companies that are dealing with the demographic shift caused by the retirement of baby boomers tend to worry most about how they will deal with the resulting workforce shortages. They miss the much more significant issue of the declining productivity that results from disengaged employees who know that their next career move will be and can only be retirement.[7] When the trajectory is defined in advance, the future has no shadow and there will be no engagement. The process of wear that accompanies the passage of time is accelerated. Mature employees do not age an enterprise; the enterprise ages them. Increasing the legal retirement age without roles that allow people to make and feel a difference only makes disengagement last longer.

Tools Put to New Purpose

The adventures of the companies we have described in this chapter illustrate attempts to satisfy multiple requirements through the hard approach of alignment: dedicating jobs to requirements (such as Mr. Reparability) or creating KPIs and metrics specific to a requirement (such as talent development at the mining company). We have seen that many of the performance requirements that a company must face can only be satisfied by fostering cooperation, *not* by creating dedicated functions, procedures, or systems in a quest for strategic alignment.

We have also learned about how to foster cooperation by creating feedback loops that extend the shadow of the future and how this involves using classical tools of management, such as career paths. When applying the simple rules, companies need not and cannot abandon all the organizational levers such as goal setting, processes, role definition, career paths, and the rest. There are no other elements to design organizations.

Indeed, there is no single lever or one magic element beyond these basic ones that can instantly produce a cultural transformation, an adaptive company, a learning organization, or any of the other models that seem so appealing. Properties such as reparability, customer centricity, flexibility, speed, and others emerge from interaction patterns that are shaped by contexts, and these are, in turn, created by the combination of organizational levers.

The simple rules use the familiar elements of structure, processes, and systems, but in a very different way. What matters are not the elements per se, but the way people integrate them into their strategies. These elements are not selected according to their supposed intrinsic pros and cons, or according to their consistency in the abstract, but according to the behaviors that become rational strategies for people when the various elements come together. In doing so, you can design work contexts with surgical accuracy, in a much more specific way than with generic structural patterns. The accuracy is not in the details of what people ought to do, but in understanding why they do what they do and the way behaviors combine to produce adaptiveness, customer centricity, and performance in general. This is why a major benefit of the simple rules is that you use much fewer elements and the ones you use are really effective. The simple rules help you choose organizational levers by approaching them both at a specific level and holistically, according to their combined effect on the context of goals, resources, and constraints from which behaviors and performance arise. This smart simplicity helps you avoid falling into the complicatedness trap hidden in best practices and in the strategic alignment sequence—more and more structures, processes, and systems that set the organization further and further adrift.

SUMMARY OF SIMPLE RULE FIVE

Increase the importance to people of what happens tomorrow as a consequence of what they do today. By making very simple changes you can manage complex requirements, while also removing organizational complicatedness. With the strategic alignment typical of the hard approach, these simple solutions—for instance, career paths—often come at the end of a sequence that starts by installing the most cumbersome changes: new structure, processes, systems, metrics, and so on. Simple and effective solutions are then impossible. You can extend the shadow of the future in four ways:

- Tighten the feedback loop by making more frequent the moments when people experience the consequence of the fit between their contributions.

- Bring the end point forward, notably, by shortening the duration of projects.

- Tie futures together so that successful moves are conditioned by contributing to the successful move of others.

- Make people walk in the shoes they make for others.

6

Simple Rule Six

Reward Those Who Cooperate

Rule six is the third of the three simple rules that impel people to best use their judgment and energy to deal with complexity. Although all three of these rules rely on the creation of feedback loops, the loops of rules four and five are direct. Rule six, by contrast, is indirect.

Sometimes, the nature of tasks and activities is such that feedback can only come indirectly—through the judgment and evaluation made by other people, usually managers—and rule six is about creating this kind of feedback loop. This type of indirect feedback loop may be necessary when there is a long time lag between causes and effects, or when jobs are so insulated from one another that people in those jobs are immune to the reciprocal impact of others' behavior.

In such cases, senior managers can close the feedback loop by following the sixth simple rule: reward people who cooperate and do not reward those who do not. To this end, managers will need to use the familiar tool of performance evaluation, although in a very different way.

In this chapter, you will learn:

- **How to move beyond using purely technical criteria in performance evaluations.** In practice, most performance evaluations are about finding technical causes for problems and identifying the people responsible to then place blame. A more effective use of performance evaluations is to foster cooperation.

- **How to make those who don't cooperate bear the cost.** People should not be blamed for failures, especially when they happen in an attempt to meet a performance requirement. Rather, people should be blamed for *failing* to help others who are in need of help.

- **How to change the managerial dialogue to make transparency a resource rather than a constraint.** Many organizations play a game of target setting that discourages transparency and prevents groups from achieving their full potential. The managerial dialogue around performance evaluation should use people's knowledge to best effect and to encourage innovation.

In this chapter, we will illustrate these points through a detailed case study of how managers at a passenger railway company we call RapidTrain changed the performance evaluation process to get its trains to run on time.

RapidTrain: Improving On-Time Performance

On-time performance used to be RapidTrain's strong suit. But over the past ten years, due to the rapid increase in traffic, on-time arrivals had declined below 80 percent. Leveraging its long history of technological excellence, the company had tried many different solutions: upgrading its traffic control systems, creating a new function to monitor delays, and rationalizing some operations such as cleaning and equipment checks. But each initiative, even if it did slightly increase on-time performance, also had a negative impact on other performance requirements, including cost, quality, and safety. Given the company's strict standards, this was unacceptable, so RapidTrain stopped each on-time improvement initiative before it could improve punctuality.

Then, competition from other railways and alternative transportation modes intensified. RapidTrain had no choice but to improve its on-time performance while also keeping to its strict standards for safety, quality, and cost. How could the company possibly do that? We suggested to the executive team members that they focus on improving cooperation instead of relying on individual accountability and adding new resources. However, many people did not see the need to improve cooperation. For instance a maintenance supervisor said: "Lack of cooperation is an excuse. If we are all accountable in our silos the trains will be on time, cooperation or not. My job is to make sure the trains leave maintenance in the right way at the right time." The hard approach. A recently hired manager responded: "Your silo-mentality is typical of the bureaucratic mind-set we find here, because of the civil servant history in a state-owned company." This was the soft approach, according to which mind-sets drive behaviors, and the only solution for sure is "to change mentalities."

The key operational units that had to cooperate with each other included maintenance staff, train drivers, conductors, and station crews. Members of the maintenance unit, for example, could immediately inform the other functions about the nature of the repairs they were going to perform and how long they would take. In turn, platform managers could then announce the delays to passengers and position them on the platform so they were ready to board as soon as the repaired train arrived; a more efficient boarding process would make up for the delay that originated in the maintenance unit. Vice versa, whenever a train arrived at the station needing maintenance, the station manager could speed things up by sending it to the platform closest to the maintenance shed. The train conductors could help the platform team manage the flow of passengers once boarding had begun. In other words, cooperation would provide a wider set of choices so that, depending on the circumstances and specific nature of the unexpected issues, RapidTrain could find a superior solution to satisfy its conflicting performance requirements.

The operational units at RapidTrain, however, had not been cooperating in the ways that were necessary to solve the on-time arrival problem. What was all the more frustrating for senior managers (and employees) was that the organization would display exceptional cooperation during crises (caused by extreme weather, for instance). In a crisis situation, the teams would quickly find ingenious solutions that were considered wonders by the usual industry standards. Putting direct feedback loops in place was not an option to achieve the same level of cooperation on a day-to-day basis. RapidTrain personnel were insulated from reciprocal impacts because of the very nature of train traffic in a large network. Members of the functions worked at numerous sites throughout the day and interacted with the various functions differently in every situation. Rule five—extending the shadow of the future—was not applicable because a maintenance worker can't become a conductor on the train he has just repaired in order to experience the consequences of his actions. A train conductor needs to be on the platform before the train arrives from maintenance, preferably with clean clothes and hands.

It was up to the management team to close the feedback loop. What performance evaluation criterion could it use to create a context within which cooperation became the best choice for team members? To answer this question, we worked with managers at RapidTrain, first to understand the existing work context. We discovered that the real goal of the unit managers was not so much to make sure the train was on time for the passengers as it was to avoid being found guilty of creating delays and getting blamed for them.

That goal had arisen as a direct result of one of the earlier measures RapidTrain had taken in an attempt to improve its on-time percentage—the creation of a new monitoring function. Whenever a train was late, the monitoring function pounced and undertook an investigation to determine which unit had caused the delay. Thousands of hours were spent in these investigations, as the monitoring function issued one finding after another, and the units rebutted them or tried to explain them away. An investigation would go on until it could reveal which unit was responsible for the technical factor that was the root cause of the delay. Had someone failed to replenish the oil stock? Had the wrong platform been announced? When the technical root cause was determined, the manager of the unit in which it occurred was pronounced guilty, with an impact on annual evaluation and promotion decisions. This approach is standard practice in the railway sector, as well as in many other businesses. Whenever there is a delay—such as a holdup in construction or a slip in the delivery of a piece of software—organizations determine the technical root cause and then place blame.

The main resources of a unit manager were the team and equipment under his or her direct control. Were the other units also a resource? Remember that nothing is a resource in itself. It depends on the actor's goal as shaped by the work context. So, yes, the other units were a secondary resource—however, not because they could help, but because they were potential candidates to get the blame when something went wrong. There was little mutual help among the functions, except during a serious crisis. To get help, one needs to ask for help. But as soon as a unit asked for help, it was signaling that it was the root cause of the delay. So when a problem happened in a unit, its manager and team would try to accelerate and make up for the delay by themselves. Sometimes that worked but not regularly enough to improve on-time performance. Delays in one function would translate into delays in the others, delaying the train and affecting the network.

Of course, no one deliberately decides to be the technical root cause for a problem. Generally, if you delay others, you don't make a deliberate choice to do so. However, when the others are delayed because they do not cooperate to help make up for the delays you have caused, they *have* made a deliberate choice not to cooperate. If someone is to be blamed, who should it be—you or the others?

We have never encountered a situation in which people were not able to cooperate. Our constant observation is that people have room to maneuver in allocating their efforts to ensure either the protection granted by their measurable contribution or the nonmeasurable contribution to overall results. The typical barrier is not unwillingness to spend more energy—people usually fully spend it anyway in protecting themselves one way or another—but the risk involved in turning an effort into nonmeasurable cooperation. At RapidTrain, the analysis showed that people were making the greatest efforts in trying to catch up and accelerate on their own, but often in vain. To be sure, being transparent with others would have required much less energy. What if all these efforts and intelligence, instead of being used in vain, could be turned toward making the trains run on time, thanks to cooperation?

Based on this analysis, RapidTrain senior management made a major change in the evaluation criteria. The executives decided that once a unit told others it had a problem, the units that failed to cooperate in solving the problem would be held responsible for the delay. To realize how radical the change was, think of it this way: it was a bit like saying, "When another unit causes you to be late, *you* are going to be the one that takes the blame." The key question was no longer: "Are you technically the cause of the delay?" It was: "Have you cooperated to solve it?" Evaluation was no longer hinging on technical criteria but rather on organizational ones.

Each week, the managers of the units sat down with their superiors to review the delays and to answer the new question. Station managers, who were present at some key moments of cooperation, also judged if units had contributed to solving problems. Of course, the senior managers also made it clear that if the same unit remained the cause of repeated problems because it did not engage in continuous improvement, it would take the blame. But there was no longer a direct link between technical causes and blame. It became in the interest of those who needed help to be transparent about it and in the interest of others to provide that help. The enhanced cooperation, in turn, allowed RapidTrain to bring further improvement to each unit's work processes.

In just four months after initiating the new approach, on-time performance at RapidTrain jumped to 95 percent on the major lines where the change had been implemented. This was achieved without new equipment, new scheduling systems, or additional trains or teams. A side benefit was that people no longer had to spend thousands of hours in the root cause investigations, as it was in everybody's interest to be transparent about his or her own problems—and also because there were fewer delays.

Another outcome was also important. As part of the evaluation of the change initiative, one team launched an employee survey and interviewed the unit members to probe how they felt about the new approach. The feedback was that they felt happier than they had before. Three factors seemed to account for this greater satisfaction at work. First, the teams in contact with customers were now able to provide more helpful answers in case of problems, while taking mitigating actions. Relationships with customers had changed for the better. Second, hierarchical relationships had improved. The managers could now help units get the cooperation they needed from others. Third, there was also some pride in breaking the records. Indeed, this is what happens when efforts are turned toward cooperation. (See the sidebar "Use Performance Evaluation to Enhance Cooperation.") Interestingly the maintenance supervisor told us when we met him again that his real role was "to make teams cooperate so that passengers, not only maintenance, arrived on time." His mind-set had changed, and without psychoanalysis or bureaucracy therapy. In fact, the context had changed, behaviors had intelligently adjusted, and mind-set had evolved as a consequence.

SIMPLE RULES TOOLKIT

Use Performance Evaluation to Enhance Cooperation

Don't punish or blame people for results but encourage in-depth knowledge of how results are obtained and who helped out.

Managerial presence and feedback loops capture how each individual contributes to the effectiveness of others, making it more difficult to pass the buck to the weak roles that bear most of the adjustment cost. Helping others with their results then becomes attractive and, in turn, fuels transparency about performance.

Do not confuse the following three terms: *business steering* (which requires many metrics and KPIs to identify and anticipate the trajectory of the business), *performance management* (evaluating people's performance by using some metrics and also your qualitative judgment, providing advice for improvement), and *rewards* (the way to gratify contributions). The balanced scorecard is often a sophisticated form of confusion among these three elements, where remuneration ends up being a direct function of the score achieved by people in performing against the weighted average of the multiple business KPIs. *The system has computed your score, and as your manager I am very happy to tell you that this year you have achieved a great 4.81—I am not surprised—for the rest, please see the accountant who has your check ready, and don't forget to celebrate!* If the manager is not surprised, what was the point in having the score? If the manager is surprised, what was the point in having the manager? It is rare that managers say they are surprised, which simplifies discussions but does not simplify the balanced scorecard, let alone the achievement of overall results.

All too often, a company chooses performance assessment criteria to link things that go well or badly in operational processes to specific areas of responsibility. The more direct, accurate, and clear the link, the more it thinks it has the right assessment system. But the proper goal of an evaluation system is not to be technically right in this link. Rather, it is to elicit full engagement and cooperation. So, in using an evaluation system, ask: "Are we trying to be true to the technicalities of the job description or trying to generate engagement and cooperation?" This question often causes managers to change the criteria, move away from technicalities, and emphasize the parts of work that make a difference.

Make Those Who Don't Cooperate Bear the Cost

One way to apply this simple rule is to adopt the principle established by Jørgen Vig Knudstorp, CEO of the LEGO Group: "Blame is not for failure, it is for failing to help or ask for help."[1] When this is the rule, people become much more transparent about their weaknesses, uncertainties in their business forecasts, and opportunities they have for improvement.

An organization is much more resilient when people know that it is in their individual interest to help others and to be transparent than when people are judged and rewarded on their ability to avoid mistakes in their own area. When people work in this way, they will always have the help of others accountable for finding the solution to a problem. This is the strength of the Musketeers' motto: "One for all and all for one."

This approach puts the vital issue of tolerance for failure in a useful perspective. Intolerance for failure is bad. It can lead to risk phobia: "Don't take initiatives. Don't try new ideas. Hide your mistakes!" Issuing a decree of zero tolerance for mistakes will not prevent them from happening. It will only cause people to hide the mistakes that do occur.

Still, tolerance for failure is not always good either, because it can often just lower the bar. The proper intent of tolerance for failure is not to provide greater leniency or make requirements less demanding. Just because people are given the right to make mistakes does not mean the eraser should be allowed to wear out faster than the pencil.

The right way to administer tolerance for failure is to use criteria that place demands where people can create the greatest impact for the organization and its performance—where individuals have a margin of maneuver that could be combined with that of others to make a big difference. By using criteria that reward decisions that would otherwise be risks for people individually, even when good for the company, pressure can be focused on the points that foster cooperation and therefore have more impact than pressure within silos. This kind of tolerance for failure makes the resulting system more tolerant of failure— that is, more robust. The result is reliability without the need to multiply control mechanisms. Attitudes toward risk are often described in terms of culture or mind-set. *Our people are risk-adverse. Our culture is not tolerant enough of risk*. This is wrong. In fact all these issues usually have nothing to do with people's particular psychology or mind-set. Most often they are organizational and practical matters of cooperation. Risk is not a goal in itself. What matters is the effect on organizational performance and individuals. Risk-taking is a good thing only when there is cooperation. Only cooperation can make risk-taking a *rational strategy* for the individual. People take personal risk when they know they can count on the cooperation of others—to compensate, relay, absorb, or provide a safety net in case things go wrong. And then risk also becomes fruitful for the company.

How does your organization administer the right to fail? Is it completely intolerant of failure? Does it verge on leniency? Or do you approach failure in a way that generates resilience?

Changing the Managerial Dialogue: Make Transparency a Resource, Not a Constraint

An important ingredient of evaluation is the dialogue that managers have with their teams. By evaluation, we mean the conversations and judgments about whether people have given their best, what helps them, and what obstructs them. (We are not referring to the boxes that have to be filled in as part of the standard annual evaluation form.) The way managers frame this conversation is important.

"What Do People Say When They Complain about You?"

A CEO we know used to begin the evaluation of his manager of shared services by asking, "I have heard some complaints from country operations about your responsiveness. What's going on?" The CEO was on a fault-finding mission. So, for the manager, it became a game of defense, countering each complaint with positive testimonials he had received from other quarters.

This approach doesn't make the best use of people's intelligence or of the available information. The CEO, who was most removed from operations, had little choice but to focus his attention on second-hand information about the manager's performance and supposed problems. The manager, in turn, had no choice but to use his intelligence to justify his performance, attack his attackers, and pump up his successes. It was not a conversation, but rather a sequence of thrusts and parries.

The CEO came to realize this approach was not leading to performance improvement and decided to change how he handled the performance evaluation. He entered the conversation differently, by asking, "What frustrations do you cause your internal clients? What do they complain about? How can I help you solve these problems? Only one thing would be inexcusable: that I hear from other people about issues involving you and I have not already heard about them from you. This would mean that I know your internal customers better than you do."

By evaluating people on their knowledge of what is not working in their area, rather than encouraging them to play personal defense, the logic of the conversation is reversed. The responsibility for supplying information and for acting on it is put on those who are best placed to do so.

This kind of dialogue can't rely on information gathered through internal customer satisfaction surveys and the like. These may provide a rank-ordered list of complaints, but they don't tell you what really matters. How, for example, does the shared services manager view these complaints? What does he make of them? Only he can understand the implications of these findings for his own processes and operations, and only he can determine what he needs to do in order to improve.

"What Personal Risk Are You Taking in All This?"

The way the performance cycle starts in many companies explains why evaluation is often performed entirely without reference to cooperation and without any understanding of context, and therefore drives underperformance. The performance cycle starts when targets are set at the start of the year.

Typically, once a year, the executive team asks line managers for their performance forecasts. This process can be repeated when there are specific needs for cost savings or top-line growth, in which case there is usually an overall ambition and performance improvement target already in place.

The negotiations begin. The executive committee sets very high targets, knowing that people will give performance forecasts lower than those they know they could actually attain. They do this to keep some concessions—something in reserve—for the next round of negotiations. They know there will be a second round, because all their colleagues will also offer low performance expectations in the first round, so the total will never add up to what the executive committee wants. The gap between ambition at the company level and the results of all the bottom-up commitments is fully anticipated.

After the second round, people raise performance expectations a little, but still set them short of what is achievable. They all know that committing to improvements, and delivering them, is going to make things even tougher next year. When the process begins again, they will have to start from a much harder place and go up from there, promising to deliver even more performance improvements, such as even more savings and even higher growth. So people keep as much as they can in reserve. Another reason people do not reveal or aim for the fullest possible improvement they believe they could attain is the risk of what others will do. Whatever you are in charge of—sales, Asia-Pacific sites, logistics, client accounts—the chances are you have some interdependencies with others. No one has total control of the outcome. If you can't count on the cooperation of others, then setting even a reasonable target makes you hostage to fate. Better to play it safe.

Perhaps even riskier is setting a target for yourself that requires something *new* to be done. Imagine if your improvement plan involves trying new approaches instead of the battle-tested solutions (for instance, selecting unknown suppliers as opposed to well-established vendors) or challenging some procedures—and you fail? The result would be to take a double hit: for not achieving your target and for not having the excuse of good compliance.

Finally, nothing bad will come of playing it safe. Quite the opposite. Performance targets become management KPIs, and KPIs determine incentives. Eventually, people will deliver more than their targets and get the maximum bonus (rewarding overperformance is common practice), while the performance improvement potentials are far from being fully exploited. In these companies, no one has an interest in being transparent about obtainable improvements, let alone those that would be a stretch.

Not only is it a rational strategy *not* to target the full potential improvement, each person knows that everyone else has the same strategy. This is all the more reason for exercising restraint on the forecasts. The collective dynamic is one of diminishing returns accompanied by great bonuses. The individual prospect of taking a double hit when taking a personal risk boomerangs into a double hit for the organization.

Now, what happens at the end-of-year review when you have promised a 1 percent improvement in your KPI but have actually obtained a 2 percent improvement? You explain it by saying, "We worked harder and were much cleverer than even we suspected we could be!" Your manager is not fooled. She wants to know why you got the forecast wrong. Why didn't you set the target at 2 percent?

Then the company goes one better: a KPI and incentive are added for the accuracy of your forecast. (Unfortunately, this is not a thought experiment in the absurd; we have seen companies do this.) Some calculations are involved, because, of course, the incentive related to accuracy of forecast must translate into more bonus than what can be gained for overdelivering by 100 percent. In light of these new developments, each manager now has to calculate what his or her new optimum individual strategy is. There are new KPIs and incentives to be considered. The game has not changed, but the organization is more complicated.

This dynamic is radically changed when a manager follows rule six by asking three questions in a one-on-one discussion with each of his or her team members:

1. What will you do to improve performance next year and what will be the results in terms of savings, product launches, or revenues?

2. What are the personal risks to you in setting up this target? For example, do you have to rely on new kinds of suppliers, try different processes, or require the cooperation of one unit or another?

3. How can I help you get the cooperation you need from others to mitigate that risk?

Now, people are impelled to break new ground because if their answer to the second question is that they are not taking any personal risks, then the conclusion is that they are not trying anything particularly ambitious. By asking the third question, the manager acts as an integrator. It is now much more attractive for team members to be transparent and to try real innovations. In so doing, they will be able to benefit from cooperation to deliver higher performance since their answer to the third question puts their manager in the position of an integrator.

This approach changes the whole game. Taking a personal risk shifts from being a losing strategy to a winning one. In companies that do not take this approach, people put the organization and its customers at risk. In the new game, however, risk is openly discussed, shared, expressed, and known by everyone. When risks are made explicit, they can be handled through collective capabilities and managed, thanks to cooperation, allowing for greater performance improvement and more innovation. It is striking to note that the dialogue about "what personal risk are you taking in this or that endeavor" is completely absent in many organizations.

The new context makes a huge difference in the way people use their intelligence and energy; efforts to hide and to protect themselves from others make way for sharing, innovating, and acting collectively to mitigate risks. Before, they used intelligence to keep performance below its potential, while triggering work-on-work (reporting, control, modifications, verifications and the like added on top of actual work) to supposedly counter this misbehavior. Now they use intelligence to push and exploit potential, and there is no need for work-on-work.

We have observed this behavior of "keeping reserves" in companies because it is the intelligent thing to do, given the way the management dialogue usually goes. People's rational behaviors adjust so effectively to the managerial dialogue that changing the terms of this dialogue over performance improvement processes will usually have a fundamental effect on company results. Remember that organizations have so many problems, not because people are stupid, but because they adjust very effectively and intelligently to the counterproductive context that management unwittingly creates. And if managers create such a counterproductive context, it is because of the ineffectiveness of the hard and soft solutions in the managerial toolbox.

Avoid the Influence of Vested Interests

Managers must always ensure that they set the terms for the best group result overall, not just when it relates to performance management. In a multinational company comprising ten major units and functions, the CEO wanted to evolve the organizational design. He had some ideas about how to reconfigure it, but also wanted to gather ideas and insights from his management team. However, there was a complication. Each member of his team headed up one of the units or functions that would inevitably be affected by an organizational change. So, because of these vested interests, the CEO worried they would have a difficult time making unbiased recommendations. How could he structure the process of organization design such that he could harness the intelligence of his management group and also ensure that the new organization would serve the interests of the overall company rather than the interests of one function or another?

The CEO gathered his management team and, in a nutshell, said, "You know our strategic challenges. You know the limitations of the ten building blocks of our organization. I would like each of you to have a go at defining what the role and decision rights of each of these ten components should be. You may also revise the blueprint and bundle together or split apart existing building blocks." Then came the most interesting part, "No matter what you recommend, each of you will remain on the management team, but I will decide later which unit or function you will be in charge of."

This is an approach very similar to what philosopher John Rawls calls making decisions behind a "veil of ignorance," to ensure that individual members contribute in the best interests of the entire group.[2] If the outcome of the choices can disadvantage any unit, then any executive could be the one to suffer the consequences. If it is made impossible to game the process to advantage your own unit's interests, then the only criterion you can use in your choice is the best interests of the group overall.

At this ten-unit multinational company, the top executives had specific knowledge of the unit they were managing and also had a good sense of how the other units operated. By creating a veil of ignorance—in this case, each executive was ignorant of where he or she would end up—the CEO got the executives to use their full knowledge with as little bias as possible.

Refuse Escalation

The idea of greater transparency in performance and richer conversations with teams about what can be improved may make some managers' hearts sink. That is because they suffer from endless escalations of decisions—that is, they spend a great deal of their time on decisions that their teams have delegated upward for arbitration. But in almost all these cases, the decision will have been escalated to these managers because the people who are doing the work have failed to cooperate in making decisions.

To avoid this problem, and indeed it is a problem, we advise an approach that may at first seem a little simplistic: refuse escalation. Rather than accept the role of arbitrator, senior managers must require that the people who failed to cooperate in the first place find a solution.

The effect of escalation can be pernicious. As decisions are escalated to higher and higher levels, the decision makers are farther from the concrete reality of the work situation and more deprived of rich and fresh information. So whenever arbitration takes place at a level above that of the real action, the decisions are bound to be of lower quality than that which could have been achieved through the direct cooperation of the people directly involved.

As a top manager, you should refuse to arbitrate. Instead, round up those who need to cooperate, put them in a room, and close the door. Let them out only once they have reached a satisfactory decision. Of course, in reality, there are likely to be times when the decision making takes so long that you will have to open the door. When this is the case, however, do so on two conditions. First, make sure you hold accountable those who were involved in the escalation: "I will remember in my evaluation how many times you drove me to make decisions you were better placed to make." Second, make it a learning experience. Ask them: "What will you do differently the next time, so I don't have to arbitrate?"

SUMMARY OF SIMPLE RULE SIX

When you cannot create direct feedback loops embedded in people's tasks, you need management's intervention to close the loop. Managers must then use the familiar tool of performance evaluation, but in a very different way.

- Managers must go beyond technical criteria (putting the blame where the root cause problem originated). In dealing with the business complexity of multiple and often conflicting performance requirements, the smart organization accepts that problems in execution happen for many reasons and that the only way to solve them is to *reduce* the payoff for all those people or units that fail to cooperate in solving a problem, even if the problem does not take place exactly in their area, and to *increase* the payoff for all when units cooperate in a beneficial way.

- They must not blame failure, but blame failing to help or ask for help.

- Instead of the elusive sophistication of balance scorecards and other counterproductive cumbersome systems and procedures, they can use simple questions to change the terms of the managerial conversation so that transparency and ambitious targets become resources rather than constraints for the individual. Managers then act as integrators by obtaining from others the cooperation that will leverage the rich information allowed by this transparency and help achieve superior results.

Conclusion

Underlying the management of today's organizations is a set of beliefs and practices—the hard and soft approaches we have discussed at length in this book—that, given the new complexity of business, have become obsolete. There is no kinder way to say it. Adhering to these obsolete approaches in trying to better manage complexity results in organizational complicatedness, which damages productivity and erodes people's satisfaction at work. It is a vicious circle. The primary goal of the simple rules is to create more value by better managing business complexity. This involves abandoning the hard and soft approaches. In doing so, you also remove complicatedness and its costs. Simplification is not a goal in itself, but a valuable by-product of the simple rules.

The simple rules are battle-proven ways to leverage state-of-the art thinking and practices from the social sciences to break the vicious circle of complicatedness, help companies grow, create enduring value, and achieve competitive advantage. Each of the preceding chapters has focused on one of the simple rules and explored its implications for managers. Now we want to look at the rules holistically to see how the insights from each can be brought together. In this section, we offer a step-by-step sequence you can follow to move away from the reliance on the hard and soft approaches and toward the use of the six simple rules. Use it when you consider engaging in organization redesign, restructuring, operating model redefinition, cultural transformation, productivity improvement, or cost reduction programs. In most cases you will solve the real issues—in a faster, simpler, and deeper way.

Step One: Use Pain Points to Discover Interdependencies and Cooperation Needs

Every organization has its own distinct pain points. These may pertain to performance:

- The on-time percentage of our trains is too low.

- The occupancy rate at our hotels is below target.

- Our time to market is too long.

- Our products aren't innovative enough.

The pain points may also pertain to people's well-being at work, which can be seen in the number of sick days, turnover rates, on-the-job accidents, and people's unhappiness expressed in survey responses.

When you look at any kind of pain point and dig sufficiently into the workings of your organization, you will discover roles that are involved in the poor performance or the unhappiness, but whose interactions—if they were cooperating and benefiting from the cooperation of others—would meet the challenge of complexity while avoiding complicatedness.

Once you have identified these roles, you must focus on their interdependencies. You need to understand the extent to which a role has an impact on the ability of others to do their job. Starting from the pain of the receptionists at InterLodge, you will understand their dependency on back-office functions. Or, starting from the poor performance of the development engineers at MobiliTele, you will discover their dependency on the transceiver unit.

One way to come to such an understanding is to ask people in each role to describe what other roles would do differently if they were cooperating. This is the application of simple rule one: understanding what people actually do. You can bring out these glimpses of an ideal world of cooperation in workshops and one-on-one discussions, or through interviews. Whatever the method, the activity enables people to gain an understanding of what cooperation would look like from the perspective of others and from the perspective of performance. To do this, people must:

- **Describe what others would do if they were cooperating.** They must talk in specifics, using action verbs, rather than in vague concepts such as "trust" or "responsiveness to others." Cooperation is a behavior, and a behavior is an action rather than an attitude or mindset. A buyer, for example, might say, "You, the category strategist, would frame contracts that give me freedom to negotiate with suppliers." Or the station platform manager would say, "Ideally, you maintenance people would tell us when, and by how much, the train is delayed."

- **Define the difference that cooperation would make.** Organizations do not seek cooperation for its own sake, but rather for the results it brings. People must describe, with specifics, the difference that cooperating would make to their individual performance and to the organization's overall results: "If you guys in procurement did what I have described, I would be able to reduce inventories by 15 percent."

If this exercise goes as it should, you will have identified key interdependencies and cooperation needs, which are the link between the solution to complexity (and, hence, the elimination of poor performance and dissatisfaction at work) and the concrete changes that the organization will need to make. Once you have identified these roles and defined the differences cooperation would make, you can focus your analysis on the changes needed to simultaneously improve performance and increase satisfaction.

Step Two: Discover Obstacles to Cooperation

You cannot immediately make these changes, however. You must first uncover the reasons why cooperation is not happening in these roles. To do so, you need the data that you can gather by working out the answers to two key questions, discussed in chapter 1:

1. *How do behaviors combine with each other to produce the current performance levels?* Think about how behaviors adjust and influence each other, given the power relationships and adjustment costs. When you ask this question and consider the answers, be careful to avoid the trap of blaming a performance issue on the *lack* of an organizational element such as a structure, process, or system. Keep in mind that the absence of one thing cannot cause the presence of something else. This "root cause-by-absence" explanation opens the door to complicatedness.

2. *What is the context of goals, resources, and constraints that makes the current behaviors "rational strategies" for people?* When you answer this question, be careful not to explain behaviors—actions, decisions, and interactions—by invoking people's mentality or mind-set. These are tautological explanations at best. They often put the guilt on the individual, or a group of individuals, while obscuring the real issues. Instead, understand what makes cooperation avoidable or counterproductive for people, in their current context of goals, resources, and constraints. A few possibilities that may make people avoid cooperation are:

   - **An abundance of resources** that remove interdependencies and fuel dysfunctional self-sufficiency.

   - **Enough power to avoid cooperating.**

- **Not enough power to take the risk of cooperating.** Some roles are so powerless that they would bear all the adjustment cost and not gain enough back in return; they are better off isolating themselves.

All the stories we have presented in this book—InterLodge, MobiliTele, RapidTrain, GrandeMart, and so on—show that an improper understanding of individual behaviors and how they combine to produce performance led companies to miss the real problem and thus take complicated, counterproductive measures.

Step Three: Capture the Benefits

Once you have understood the context that shapes behaviors and thus affects performance, you are in a good position to change that context.

Change the Context

Use the simple rules as guidelines to identify ways to change the context of goals, resources, and constraints so that full engagement and cooperation become individually useful for those involved, as follows:

- **Simple rule one: Understand what your people do.** This rule adds an understanding of context to the manager's resources.

- **Simple rule two: Reinforce integrators.** This rule reinforces managers as integrators by removing some of their constraints (such as bureaucratic rules, intermediary roles, and coordinating functions) and increasing their resources (such as room of maneuver and discretionary power). It adds to employees' resources by allowing them to benefit from the cooperation of others.

- **Simple rule three: Increase the total quantity of power.** This rule adds resources to those who currently disengage and avoid cooperation because they have more to lose than to win by coming out of isolation. They are provided with new power bases derived from the control of important stakes.

- **Simple rule four: Increase reciprocity.** This rule changes goals or problems by defining rich objectives and removes the resources that create internal monopolies or fuel dysfunctional self-sufficiency.

- **Simple rule five: Extend the shadow of the future.** This rule transposes remote consequences into people's goals today and turns insufficient cooperation into a constraint for those who do not cooperate.

- **Simple rule six: Reward those who cooperate.** This rule makes it individually useful for everybody to be transparent about, and to exploit, all possibilities for improving performance.

As seen in the previous chapters, the practical implementation of the simple rules to create the right context entails changing various aspects of the organization such as budgeting, invest-ment, objective setting, information systems, evaluation and reward criteria, career paths, the scope of roles and decision rights, hierarchical links and layers, recruiting and training for new skills, and others. These solutions use the classical building blocks of organization. The key difference is that you will end up only with those necessary and sufficient to deal with business complexity.

Before cracking open the champagne, however, you need to do something else: commit to the performance improvement that can now be realized as a result of the new context.

Raise Ambitions

In step one, you asked people to describe the positive impact that cooperation would have on results and they responded with specifics—"I could cut my inventories by 15 percent if procure-ment would . . ."—and they also agreed on the ways to make cooperation happen.

Based on those conversations, it now makes sense to upgrade performance targets: 15 percent lower inventory levels (or shorter time to market, increased sales levels, improved customer satis-faction, and so on).

Sometimes people will not spontaneously or immediately agree to these commitments. Don't worry. You can always go back to the drawing board: "Did we exaggerate or make mistakes when we first projected performance improvements based on cooperation from others? Did we overlook some obstacles or solutions?" Because of the contexts set up by the six simple rules, there is nothing potentially complacent in these conversations. They are all opportunities to better understand reality.

Your action plan has three important features:

- **Problems are depersonalized.** No individual or group is made to feel guilty because of personal traits or psychology. All understand that the work context is the issue, not any one person or group. This approach removes the obstacles to change that would be triggered by the denial (of the diagnostic, of the root causes, and so on) of those who would otherwise feel under personal attack.

- **Change is not anxiety-provoking.** Any changes proposed will not have come out of the blue or be conceived in an ivory tower. They will not be threatening, because everyone knows they address real issues. This removes the obstacles to change relating to misunderstanding.

- **Buy-in is built in.** It will not be necessary to sell the solution at all costs via corporate communication campaigns (or compromises) once its design has been finalized. Because solutions are developed in full knowledge of the context— why people do what they do—they incorporate the conditions for successful implementation.

By discovering together how cooperation can improve their performance, people create a context in which they enable and impel each other to realize these improvements. (See the sidebar "Three Steps from Pain to Performance.")

SIMPLE RULES TOOLKIT

Three Steps from Pain to Performance

1. Mutual Discovery of Where and Why Cooperation Matters for Results

- Where are the pain points in performance and in satisfaction at work?
- How does each function affect the ability of others to do what they have to do?
- What would effective cooperation look like from each actor's perspective?
- What difference would it make on each actor's results and overall performance?

2. Joint Diagnosis of Obstacles

- What are the differences between what happens and the ideal cooperation we have described?
- Why do people do what they do?

3. Co-definition of Changes and Resulting Higher Ambitions

- How can we use the simple rules to change the context so that cooperation becomes individually useful (a *rational strategy*) for people?
- What enhanced targets can each of us then commit to?

The Day-to-Day Battle against "Best Practices"

To improve performance by managing complexity while avoiding complicatedness, you will find yourself up against the decades-long accretion of business theory that has turned management into an abstraction and that has abstracted management from its real job.

As we have seen, some of the abstractions will typically creep in around the following:

- **Reporting lines.** Endless arguments may occur about the pros and cons of different types of reporting lines—full, dotted, or bold—as if the dotted line has dotted power to obtain dotted behaviors, and fuller behavior is achieved by the fuller power of the fuller line.

- **KPIs.** You may find yourself mired in debates about the respective weight that each of your fifteen or twenty KPIs should have, as if by getting the right weighting and associated incentives, behaviors will end up precisely where the weighted average of the formula lies.

- **Leadership styles.** The organization may deliberate on the mix of leadership styles needed in the management team. The assumption seems to be that it can decree leadership styles to leaders in place or import them by recruiting people who supposedly embody those styles, while, in fact, people adjust their style (the way they do what they do) to their context.

While these abstractions may be intellectually seductive, they are deceptive in practice. An intellectual organization is not the same as one that harnesses the intelligence of its people. To create that kind of organization requires an authentic presence of management as well as material feedback loops such as those we have described here. To have an authentic management presence, you have to regain direct knowledge of operations and escape the abstractions and symbols that are meant to represent work—structures, procedures, KPIs, and the rest—but that push management to the periphery of work.

Do not accept this fate. You do not have to live in a world of abstractions. You need not spend your time wracking your brain about how best to reshuffle the boxes or draw the lines in the org chart. You can deal with the real content of the work, rather than just its container, by constantly and relentlessly asking simple questions:

- What role do you expect this manager to play?

- What value is the manager supposed to add?

- What is the manager supposed to make people do that they would not spontaneously do? (Remember this is how managers add value. When people spontaneously do what they need to do, then there is no need for managers.)

- What power basis will the manager have?

The more organizations harness the power of digital technologies, disperse globally, and operate in virtual teams, the more we need to shed light on what has become increasingly obscured: the actual work real people do. Connecting to the materiality of work is both challenging and essential. Understanding the context within which work happens is a way to see the reality, which is precisely what is filtered out or obscured by visions of the supposed pros and cons of structures, processes, and systems (the hard approach) as well as stories about personalities and sentiments that turn against people (the soft approach).

This return to work on the part of management is not an intellectual or philosophical pursuit. It is a practical effort to understand the way people get things done so that you can help them make the most of their judgment and energy. Nor is this management presence a form of micromanagement or a quest for the kind of control that the hard and soft approaches supposedly make possible. Such attempts at controlling the individual become all the more damaging as business complexity increases and only fuel complicatedness. The greater the business complexity, the more you need to rely on people's judgment. The six simple rules show that such reliance can be much more than just an act of faith; it is a reasoned course where your intelligence and energy will make a difference.

Notes

Introduction

1. These simple rules were first published in Yves Morieux, "Smart Rules: Six Ways to Get People to Solve Problems Without You," *Harvard Business Review*, September 2011, pp. 78–86.

2. The BCG Institute for Organization counted these performance requirements by means of a content analysis of annual reports. We measured and compared the frequency with which different kinds of performance requirements were mentioned as part of the goals, targets, and challenges described in the reports. The complexity index is the average across all companies of the number of performance requirements, set at base 100 in 1955.

3. The BCG Institute for Organization calculated this index using regression and main-components analysis (the Partial Least Square Path Modeling, or PLS-PM, algorithm). The algorithm was applied to organizational elements such as the number of procedures, vertical layers, interface structures, coordination bodies, scorecards, and decision approvals across the surveyed sample of companies.

The effect of the increase of complicatedness is not only striking for the top quintile. On average, the proportion of people spending more than fourteen hours per week in meetings has more than doubled over the past fifteen years to 40 percent. And these people consider over half of this time to be useless. The time spent per month writing reports has also increased by 40 percent on average. The number of e-mails received per day has increased threefold in this period, while the proportion of e-mails with ten or more recipients has more than doubled. On average, people receive thirty-five internal e-mails a day that they find useless. In this period, the number of interface roles people considered useless has doubled, on average.

4. Based on our analysis, size explains only 0.0001 percent of complicatedness, and the diversity of activities explains only 0.0002 percent.

5. The BCG Institute for Organization found that the negative relationship between complicatedness and people's sense of engagement at work (negative 0.606) is stronger than the positive relationship between engagement and the *combined* effect of factors that are intended to mitigate problems at work, such as caring leadership, participative management style, strong friendships, and mutual support at work (positive 0.533). The analysis uses the ten-year proprietary BCG "Engaging for Results (EFR)" survey, which has been administered to client populations since 2002, with more than 1 million survey responses from 229 companies in 85 countries. We are not suggesting that structures, processes, or systems are more significant than the soft factors in shaping morale. We do believe, however, that we must stop underestimating the effect of organizational complicatedness. This is especially important because the soft approach only treats the symptoms—particularly people's psychological and emotional states—rather than getting at the root cause. The effect of structural complicatedness on employees' morale was identified more than a half century ago by James C. Worthy. Since then, however, it has been largely neglected. Based on his study of several different units in various geographic locations of Sears, Roebuck and Co., Worthy established the negative effect of a complicated organization—notably the number of vertical layers and burdensome coordination devices—on "both operating efficiency and employee morale." See James C. Worthy, "Organizational Structure and Employee Morale," *American Sociological Review* 15, no. 2 (April 1950): 169–179.

6. The percentage of Americans satisfied at work was 45.3 in 2009 and 42.6 in 2010. There is an obvious downward trend since 1987, the first year the survey was conducted, interrupted by periodical "bumps," in The Conference Board's words, every two to three years. See Rebecca Ray and Thomas Rizzacasa, *Job Satisfaction: 2012 Edition*, The Conference Board, Research Report TCB-R-1495-12-RR, June 2012. According to Gallup surveys, only 28 percent of the US workforce is engaged at work, the rest being actively disengaged or "merely" not engaged. In Europe, the highest scores for engagement do not exceed 23 percent (Switzerland and Austria). Surveys show similar results for Japan and Australia. See "The State of the Global Workplace," Gallup Consulting, 2011, http://www.gallup.com/strategicconsulting/145535/State-Global-Workplace-2011.aspx.

7. See Robert T. Golembiewski, Robert F. Munzenrider, and Jerry G. Stevenson, *Stress in Organizations—Toward a Phase Model of Burnout* (New York: Praeger, 1986); and David Courpasson and Jean-Claude Thoenig, *When Managers Rebel* (Basingstoke, UK: Palgrave Macmillan, 2010).

8. Productivity is the ultimate arbiter of our standard of living. Nobel prize-winning economist Paul Krugman makes it clear: "Productivity isn't everything, but in the long run it is almost everything." See Paul Krugman, *The Age of Diminished Expectations* 3rd ed. (Cambridge, MA: MIT Press, 1990, 1997), p. 11. In the United States, thanks to productivity improvements in the fifties, sixties, and early seventies, each generation was almost twice as well off as the preceding one. But productivity growth since then has suffered a long deceleration, interrupted only by a brief rebound around 2000 followed by a period of higher volatility. Since 1995, Japan's productivity growth has been about half what it was in the period 1973 to 1995. Across the fifteen largest European economies, productivity growth has declined by more than a third in each decade since the seventies. One consequence is an attempt to protect standards of living by taking on more debt, with all the risks—at the financial, economic, and social levels—that overleveraging entails.

9. For instance, the Australian Institute of Management reported in its 2010 survey of more than three thousand managers that 36 percent said they could put in more effort but instead were being "lazy" because they are "unhappy" in their jobs. See "Unhappy Managers Admit Slacking Off," Australian Institute of Management, November 30, 2010, http://www .abc.net.au/news/stories/2010/11/30/3079939.htm.

10. See "Hating What You Do," *The Economist*, October 8, 2009, http://www.economist.com/businessfinance/displaystory.cfm?story_ id=14586131.

11. Scientific management was pioneered by the works of Taylor and Henri Fayol at the start of the twentieth century. But it should be said that Taylor based his new way of management on actual observations of what workers did. He realized that misbehaviors such as soldiering and slacking off were a consequence of the poor organization of work—based on craft traditions at odds with the demands of mass production—and not of the workers' ill-will or lack of commitment. This realization of the interplay between how work is organized and the resulting behaviors was at the heart of the new principles put forward by scientific management. Fayol based his way of administering and managing firms on his own experience of reviving a failing company. Despite all the limitations of scientific management to deal with the new complexity of business, illustrations of which abound in this book, there was something very valuable in Taylor's approach: paying attention to people's work, what they really do. As Peter Drucker made clear, this is precisely what we have forgotten, but it is the primary and timeless lesson of Taylor.

12. The human relations movement unfolded in the wake of Elton Mayo's work on the so-called Hawthorne studies at Western Electric in the late 1920s. The seminal account of the Hawthorne studies is F. J. Roethlisberger and W. J. Dickson, *Management and the Worker: An Account of a Research Program Conducted by the Western Electric Company, Hawthorne Works, Chicago* (Cambridge, MA: Harvard University Press, 1939). The initial impetus for the human relations movement was to better control the "human factor" that Taylor seemed to have tackled in an overly mechanistic way. The goal was to further improve performance viewed as a by-product of positive feelings and friendly interpersonal relationships within the informal group. At the root of the human relations movement is the desire to save the workers from themselves. This desire relies on the more or less explicit assumption that employees are fundamentally irrational and that their behaviors are driven by emotional stimuli that have to be contained, channeled, and thus controlled. See, notably, Kyle Bruce and Chris Nyland, "Elton Mayo and the Deification of Human Relations," *Organization Studies* 32, no. 3 (March 2011): 383–405. In that case, it is not the financial stimuli that are supposed to trigger alignment (as in scientific management), but the emotional stimuli pulled forth by managers bestowed with the appropriate leadership style. In both scientific management and human relations, there is a Pavlovian view of behaviors: what matters is finding the right stimuli, be they financial or emotional. How to best mobilize people's intelligence is not the issue in either. The long-lived success of the human relations approach, despite its lack of robust analytical ground, has been explained by the fact that it flatters management and justifies the use of the most comfortable levers available: as Michael Rose has written, "What, after all, could be more appealing than to be told that one's subordinates are non-logical; that their uncooperativeness is a frustrated urge to collaborate; that their demands for cash mask a need for your approval; and that you have a historic destiny as a broker of social harmony?" See Michael Rose, *Industrial Behaviour: Theoretical Development Since Taylor* (Harmondsworth, UK: Penguin, 1975), p. 124. This form of applied psychology provides management with a license to address the human factor and treat particular psychological traits.

13. Cooperation is often used synonymously with coordination or collaboration. But there is a difference in meaning between these three terms, and that difference is not inconsequential. Collaboration is about teamwork as people get along, based on feelings and good interpersonal

relationships. As we will see, such relationships often lead to the avoidance of real cooperation in the interest of maintaining convivial relations within the group or team. The legacy of the human relations approach, with its soft initiatives and focus on bonding in the informal group, can only, at best, encourage collaboration. Coordination refers to allocating an order of some sort among predefined activities that have to be made compatible. Scientific management can only, at best, obtain coordination by means of procedures, interface structures, metrics, and incentives. Cooperation, by contrast, involves directly taking into account the needs of others in creating a joint output. As is often the case, the best way to see the difference in concepts is to go back to their origins. The three notions have distinct Latin roots. Collaboration refers to *co-laborare*, working side by side. The emphasis is on the proximity in the action, neighborly relationships, and there is no notion of output. Cooperation relates to *co-opera*, which is about sharing an opus; there is a clear emphasis on joint goal, output, and result. Cooperation contains a notion of shared intentionality: we define objectives together and share the outcome. However, as we will see in chapter 1 with the concept of adjustment costs, contributions and sharing may be imbalanced to a certain extent. Coordination comes from *co-ordo* (the sharing of a rank) and relates to setting an order in terms of sequence and/or importance among decisions, actions, or resources. Cooperation is a generative interaction, inasmuch as it allows for the emergence of new capabilities to handle the complexity of more numerous, fast-changing, and contradictory requirements. Coordination and collaboration are only allocative interactions: allocating an order, a favor, and so on. See Yves Morieux, "To Boost Productivity, Try Smart Simplicity," *BCG Perspectives*, July 2011, http://www.bcgperspectives.com. The kind of interactions that are central to cooperation, notably in dealing with weak signals, are explored further in Yves Morieux, Mark Blaxill, and Vladislav Boutenko, "Generative Interactions: The New Source of Competitive Advantage," in *Restructuring Strategy: New Networks and Industry Challenges*, eds. Karen O. Cool, James E. Henderson, and René Abate (Oxford, UK: Blackwell, 2005), pp. 86–110.

14. The increase in contradictory performance requirements makes it more and more elusive to predefine and specify the "right" behaviors. This fact constitutes a specification uncertainty for the hard approach. On the other hand, growing specialization entails a multiplication of interdependencies between the specialized functions. These interdependencies

make individual behaviors less directly controllable through structures, processes, and systems (because the behavior of one depends on the behaviors of others), which constitutes a programming uncertainty. Each person partly "controls"—influences and shapes—the behavior of others in a way that escapes the direct control intended by structures, processes, and systems. Interdependencies create "noise" and disturbances for the hard approach. The two uncertainties together undermine an approach to organization design that focuses on structures, processes, and systems instead of focusing on what people really do and how they mobilize their intelligence at work. The result is an organization whose output is often opposite to the intents and efforts of its members. For instance, hospitals in which the staff genuinely cares for patients, and in which structures, processes, and systems are all dedicated to caring for patients, can still be hospitals that treat patients poorly and even hurt and infect them.

15. On the theme of simplification, see Alan Siegel and Irene Etzkorn, *Simple: Conquering the Crisis of Complexity* (New York: Hachette/Twelve, 2013); and Ken Segall, *Insanely Simple: The Obsession That Drives Apple's Success* (New York: Portfolio, Penguin Group, 2012).

16. Herbert A. Simon, "A Behavioral Model of Rational Choice," *Quarterly Journal of Economics* 69, no. 1 (1955): 99–118; Michel Crozier, *The Bureaucratic Phenomenon* (Chicago: University of Chicago Press, 1964); Thomas C. Schelling, *Micromotives and Macrobehavior,* rev. ed. (New York: Norton, 1978, 2006); and Robert Axelrod, *The Evolution of Cooperation*, rev. ed. (New York: Basic Books, 1984, 2006). Another seminal work is Graham Allison and Philip Zelikow, *Essence of Decision: Explaining the Cuban Missile Crisis*, 2nd ed. (New York: Addison Wesley Longman, 1999). We should also mention the work of Richard Cyert, James March, Philip Selznick, Oliver Williamson, Rosabeth Moss Kanter, Erhard Friedberg, Jeffrey Pfeffer, François Dupuy, and Jean-Claude Thoenig. The cross-fertilization of these developments constitutes modern organizational analysis in organizational sociology. A thorough account of organizational analysis and its multiple branches is given in Erhard Friedberg (ed.), *The Multimedia Encyclopedia of Organization Theory*, DVD (Paris: R&O Multimedia, 2011). The first three simple rules draw on the notion of power and strategic analysis in organizational sociology. The last three simple rules particularly draw on game theory, and their titles are inspired by Axelrod's writings. These last three rules build on rather than mirror Axelrod's seminal writing. For instance, the concept of multiplexity for networks of interactions, explained in chapter 4, is not part of Axelrod's framework.

17. The way we use the term "rationality" in this book is based on Herbert Simon's concept of "bounded rationality." According to this idea, people do not act on the basis of an exhaustive and consistent cost-benefit analysis of their options because they do not have access to all information and cannot process it all, and their preferences may be changing or even contradictory. Their rationality is bounded, that is, relative to their context of goals and perceived resources and constraints. People use their intelligence to adapt to this context. It is in this sense that organizational sociology, in the wake of Simon's work and developments in the field of game theory, analyzes behaviors as rational strategies.

18. See Daniel H. Pink, *Drive: The Surprising Truth About What Motivates Us* (New York: Riverhead Books, 2011); and Adam M. Grant, *Give and Take: A Revolutionary Approach to Success* (New York: Viking Adult, 2013).

Chapter One

1. Just because we use the word "nudge," do not confuse our approach with a stream of thought found in public policy, for instance as described in Richard H. Thaler and Cass R. Sunstein, *Nudge: Improving Decisions About Health, Wealth, and Happiness* (New Haven, CT: Yale University Press, 2008). The difference between this approach and ours is that we look not only at individual rationality and behavior, but also at how individual behaviors adjust to each other and combine to produce collective outcomes that do not boil down to the addition of individual motives and conducts.

2. For a more detailed description of this framework, see Yves Morieux and Robert Howard, "Strategic Workforce Engagement: Designing the Behavior of Organizations for Competitive Advantage," The Boston Consulting Group, discussion paper, August 2000, http://www.bcgperspectives.com.

3. For more detail on this topic, see Yves Morieux, "Management: A Sociological Perspective" in Erhard Friedberg (ed.), *The Multimedia Encyclopedia of Organization Theory*, DVD (Paris: R&O Multimedia, 2011); and Erhard Friedberg, "Local Orders: Dynamics of Organized Action," *Monographs in Organizational Behavior and Industrial Relations*, vol. 19 (London: Jai Press, 1997).

4. See Eldar Shafir, "Introduction," in *The Behavioral Foundations of Public Policy*, ed. Eldar Shafir (Princeton, NJ: Princeton University Press, 2013), pp. 1–9.

Chapter Two

1. Indeed, some airlines have tried to create the equivalent of a rule book for pilots in the form of a standard employment contract that specified the desired behaviors of a pilot. But according to a report in *Slate*, management discovered that "formal contracts can't fully specify what it is that 'doing your job properly' constitutes for an airline pilot. The smooth operation of an airline requires the active cooperation of skilled pilots who are capable of judging when it does and doesn't make sense to request new parts and who conduct themselves in the spirit of wanting the airline to succeed." See Matthew Yglesias, "Friends Don't Let Friends Fly American Airlines," *Slate*, October 1, 2012, http://www.slate.com/blogs/moneybox/2012/10/01/don_t_fly_american_airlines_conflict_with_pilot_s_union_is_destroying_american_airlines_service_quality_and_you_have_to_stay_away_.html.

2. For more on this subject, see Yves Morieux, "The Hotel Clerk," *BCG Perspectives*, December 2005, http://www.bcgpersectives.com.

3. Based on a talk by Christine Arron and Yves Morieux at a BCG seminar on collective efficiency, March 8, 2004. Thanks to colleague Mathieu Ménégaux for his insights on cooperation in athletics. The French team consisted of Patricia Girard, Muriel Hurtis, Sylviane Félix, and Christine Arron. The US team consisted of Angela Williams, Chryste Gaines, Inger Miller, and Torri Edwards. Bronze went to Russia. Based on the personal 100-meter best of each runner, the aggregate time for the US team over 400 meters is 43.59 seconds vs. 43.95 seconds for the French team. Of course the actual relay race takes much less time, notably because runners begin their leg already running (except the first one). Based on the 100-meter best performance for each of the US and French runners for that year, the aggregate time for the US team is 44.10 seconds vs. 44.82 seconds for the French. In terms of individual speed the US team is faster. But during the 2003 final it took the French team 41.78 seconds to run the relay race, and 41.83 seconds for the US team. The French were collectively faster. To watch the race go to YouTube and search for "2003 World Athletics Champs Women's 4 × 100 m. relay final."

4. Anita Elberse with Sir Alex Ferguson, "Ferguson's Formula," *Harvard Business Review*, October 2013, pp. 116–125.

Chapter Three

1. The control of uncertainties as the origin of power is well described in Michel Crozier and Erhard Friedberg, *Actors and Systems: The Politics of Collective Action*, trans. Arthur Goldhammer (Chicago: University of Chicago Press, 1977, 1980). A seminal article on the theme of power from the managerial literature is by sociologist Rosabeth Moss Kanter, "Power Failure in Management Circuits," *Harvard Business Review*, July–August 1979, pp 65–75. The power factors analyzed by Kanter constitute uncertainties controlled by power holders. For example, if the "variety of task" is a source of power, it is because those in charge of these tasks control a greater uncertainty (a greater range of possible outcomes) for the rest of the organization than those in charge of tasks with less variety. Very often, when people enjoy tasks with greater variety it is not so much because of some kind of psychological need or dislike of boring uniformity. It is much more concrete: the power they derive from controlling a greater uncertainty allows them to advantageously negotiate their situation with the rest of the organization. The terms of exchange between them and the organization are more favorable and they can obtain more in return (better conditions, more indulgence, and so on).

2. For more on this theme, which is known as "the paradox of absolute dependency," see Yves Morieux, "Resistance to Change or Error in Change Strategy?" in Erhard Friedberg (ed.), *The Multimedia Encyclopedia of Organization Theory*, DVD (Paris: R&O Multimedia, 2011).

3. See Martin Reeves, Mike Deimler, Yves Morieux, and Ron Nicol, "Adaptive Advantage," *BCG Perspectives*, January 2010, http://www.bcgperspectives.com.

4. See André Beaufre, *Introduction to Strategy* (New York: Praeger, 1965).

Chapter Four

1. It is precisely this positive impact of each one's behavior on the contribution of others to the output that makes cooperation create what is called a supermodular production function in economics. In that case, the production function can't be broken down into an addition of separate contributions that could be measured. In the simplest terms, the whole is worth more than the sum of its parts. This nonseparability is at the root of the metering problem described by Armen A. Alchian and Harold Demsetz, "Production, Information Costs, and Economic Organization," *American*

Economic Review 62 (December 1972): 777–795. The theme is developed in the excellent book by John Roberts, *The Modern Firm* (Oxford, UK: Oxford University Press, 2004). Game theory considers supermodularity from the perspective of incentives and calls this phenomenon a strategic complementarity: one agent's decision increases the incentives of others to do something. But the word "incentives" is misleading. The whole issue with cooperation is that what one does in one's task increases the effectiveness of others in their own tasks. Pierre-Joseph Proudhon already had the intuition of supermodularity of cooperation as the basis for economic profit when he wrote: "Two hundred grenadiers stood the obelisk of Luxor [in 1836 in the center of the Place de la Concorde in Paris] upon its base in a few hours; do you suppose that one man could have accomplished a same task in two hundred days?" Proudhon went on to suggest that capitalist accounting would pay for two hundred grenadiers working one day the same as for a grenadier working two hundred days, even though the results are not the same. This difference is the basis of economic profit, the flip side of the laborer's *spoliation* in Proudhon's view. See Pierre-Joseph Proudhon, *What Is Property?* trans. Benjamin R. Tucker (New York: Dover, 1840, 1970).

2. For a detailed description of the negative impact of internal monopolies on R&D productivity in the biopharmaceutical sector, see Peter Tollman, Yves Morieux, Jeanine Kelly Murphy, and Ulrik Schulze, "Can R&D Be Fixed? Lessons from Biopharma Outliers," *BCG Focus*, September 2011, http://www.bcgperspectives.com.

3. We can certainly work much longer, and we often do. The share of employees working forty-nine hours or more per week increased by 40 percent from 1980 to 2000 in the United States (employed population, except in agriculture). (Source: Bureau of Labor Statistics employment database.) A study of US male employees (not self-employed) aged twenty-five to sixty-four showed that, in the highest earnings quintile, the share of employees working fifty hours or more per week has more than doubled from 1980 to 2000 (Peter Kuhn and Fernando Lozano, "The Expanding Workweek? Understanding Trends in Long Work Hours Among US Men, 1979–2004," no. w11895, National Bureau of Economic Research, 2005).

4. For more on this concept, see Etienne Wenger and William M. Snyder, "Communities of Practice: The Organizational Frontier," *Harvard Business Review*, January 2000, pp. 139–145.

5. The power of face-to-face interactions was described by Erving Goffman in his seminal article, "On Face-work: An Analysis of Ritual Elements of Social Interaction," *Psychiatry: Journal for the Study of Interpersonal Processes* 18 (1955): 213–231.

Chapter Five

1. That structure follows strategy was originally a historical observation of Alfred Chandler in the early 1960s. This observation progressively became a prescription that structures, processes, and systems had to be designed as alignment devices. See, for instance, Robert S. Kaplan and David P. Norton, *The Balanced Scorecard: Translating Strategy into Action* (Boston: Harvard Business School Press, 1996); and also their *Alignment: Using the Balanced Scorecard to Create Corporate Synergies* (Boston: Harvard Business School Press, 2006). The same alignment function has also been prescribed to information systems, as discussed by Yves Morieux and Ewan Sutherland, "The Interaction between the Use of Information Technology and Organizational Culture," *Behaviour and Information Technology* 7, no. 2 (1988): 205–213; and also Ewan Sutherland and Yves Morieux, eds., *Business Strategy and Information Technology* (London: Routledge, 1991).

2. The mechanistic model assumes as many parts in the machine as there are requirements that it has to satisfy: N parts for N requirements. Each of the N parts has to coordinate with the $N - 1$ other parts so there are $N(N - 1)/2$ coordination needs. We know that the number of requirements has increased by a factor of 6 over the past 55 years. Today there are $6N$ requirements rather than N. Our mechanistic model becomes $6N(6N - 1)/2$. This is 36 times its original value, plus something more or less negligible depending on the initial situation.

3. A company's IT department often has a holistic perspective on the company's information, roles, and capabilities from which an efficient and effective organizational solution could be derived *before* structures, processes, and system functionality are set. Because IT comes into the picture only toward the end of the alignment process, however, there is little room for maneuver to come up with inspired solutions. For example, IT can be used to facilitate the cooperation between specialized roles, thus removing the need for an additional coordinating layer such as the project manager. Indeed, the new frontier of IT is to improve collective productivity by being a force for cooperation. See Yves Morieux (BCG), *IT Is a Force of Cooperation*, video, http://www.dailymotion.com/video/xgfcnb_yves-morieux-bcg-l-it-est-une-force-de-cooperation_tech; and Yves Morieux, Mark Blaxill, and Vladislav Boutenko, "Generative Interactions: The New Source of Competitive Advantage," in *Restructuring Strategy: New Networks and Industry Challenges*, eds. Karen O. Cool, James E. Henderson, and René Abate (Oxford, UK: Blackwell, 2005), pp. 86–110. Instead of just attempting to improve individual productivity and

cut transaction costs, IT systems must be used to fuel the generative value of interactions and improve collective productivity.

4. For more on this theme, see Yves Morieux, "Knowledge: The Basis of Adaptive Advantage," in *Management in the Knowledge Economy: New Managerial Models for Success*, eds. Ludovic Dibiaggio and Pierre-Xavier Meschi (Paris: Pearson, 2012).

5. In many cases either the incentive is too weak and has no effect or the incentive is significant, in which case the individual's problem becomes to earn the incentives rather than doing his or her job (which always contains more than metrics can capture). Therefore the incentive either is useless or pushes the individual to deviate from the optimal solution to the job's problems. The rational behavior becomes to hide, work around, or even cheat in order to earn the incentive. Hence the need for more rules and controls. This is why simple rules four and five are so important: feedback loops are directly embedded in the tasks and activities and directly gratify or penalize people, depending on whether they do well or not. The rules create a context that makes it individually useful for people to do what they have to do. As you will see, simple rule six involves indirect feedback loops based on management evaluation, but the rule changes the context so that being transparent instead of hiding or workarounds becomes a rational behavior for people.

6. After working in the after-sales network, some engineers would then move to a new role, typically in marketing, while others would go back to engineering in a job with more responsibilities. The length of stay in the after-sales network varied according to these situations and also according to the engineer's age and seniority, but usually ranged from three to five years. A few stayed longer and even progressed through the after-sales organization.

7. Our research shows that a company with an age pyramid similar to that of the US workforce can regain the engagement of those over forty-five by extending the shadow of the future. They can also use one-fifth of the time of workers over fifty-two to reduce the ramp-up period of junior workers by 5 percent. In doing so, productivity would likely increase by more than 8 percent. See Yves Morieux, "The Unretired," *BCG Perspectives*, February 2007, http://www.bcg.com.

Chapter Six

1. Jørgen Vig Knudstorp said this to Yves Morieux on June 17, 2011, as we were discussing simple rule six. We thank him for his permission.

2. John Rawls, *A Theory of Justice* (Cambridge, MA: Belknap Press, 1971).

Index

Acknowledgments

Yves Morieux: I am grateful to the late Michel Crozier, whose passion inspired me when I was a student at the Institut d'Études Politiques in Paris and later in our joint work together. My thanks also to Michael Baker for advising me to study industrial markets from the perspective of decision analysis when I was a student at Strathclyde University in Glasgow. I am grateful, too, to Carl Stern and Rafael Cerezo for their encouragement when they were, respectively, Boston Consulting Group CEO and BCG Europe chairman, and to Hans-Paul Buerkner, current BCG chairman, for creating the fellowship program that provided BCG's Institute for Organization with the resources to understand and tackle the evolution of complexity. Thanks also to Olivia Davies, organization analyst at the Institute, for her dedication in helping reconcile research data and manuscript text. I am indebted to my BCG colleagues for their ideas and their willingness to work with me on the research and cases described in this book—thank you one and all. I wish to thank the men and women who worked with me across more than forty countries and five hundred client companies. I also thank my uncle, Emmanuel Saurin, a great business leader who taught me so much, and my parents Charles and Lydia who inspired me.

Peter Tollman: This book is dedicated to my loving parents, Ted and Shirley, architect and psychologist, who, through their own passions and perspectives, imbued in me a lifelong yearning for meaning, aesthetics, and symmetry. My fascination with behavioral dynamics as a driver of organizational effectiveness derives from these factors. My closest laboratory has been my own home, held together by my wonderful wife, Linda, and two exceptional daughters, Jess and Sarah. These three women have graciously supported and encouraged the peculiarities of my work habits and, through thoughtful criticism and lively debate, have added their unique wisdom to my thinking. Finally, the Boston Consulting Group is both a highly effective organization in itself and the best learning environment one could hope for. I'm deeply grateful for my years with BCG and for the support I've received along the way from colleagues too numerous to mention.

<hr>

Together, we wish to express our deepest gratitude to John Butman. John has followed the formation of these ideas for many years and also helped, through his patience and collaboration, make this book a reality. We are also indebted to BCG's editor-in-chief, Simon Targett, who kept the book on track despite the many obstacles consulting work puts in the way of writing. We want to thank BCG's Bob Howard, whose editing insights were invaluable at critical stages. We also want to assure the five anonymous peer reviewers of the manuscript that they have our gratitude for their insightful remarks, encouragement, and thoroughness. Melinda Merino, executive editor of Harvard Business Review Press, in her tactful yet firm direction, made sure that the necessary and sufficient points came through clearly in the book; thank you, Melinda. Rich Lesser, as BCG CEO, and Andrew Dyer and Grant Freeland, the former and current BCG People and Organization Practice leaders, are also deserving of our deepest thanks for their continuous support.

About the Authors

Yves Morieux is a senior partner and managing director in the Washington, DC, office of The Boston Consulting Group (BCG). As director of the BCG Institute for Organization and a BCG Fellow, he divides his time between leading research and advising senior executives of multinational corporations and public-sector entities in the United States, Europe, and Asia-Pacific on their strategies and organizational transformations.

Yves has contributed to the development of organization theory relating to the behavioral and structural conditions for economic value creation and competitive advantage. Turning these insights into practice with the simple rules, he has helped CEOs with their most critical challenges, for instance, moving their companies from quasi bankruptcy to industry leadership, or transforming the business model and culture to reach new heights, or successfully managing groundbreaking innovations.

Yves serves on the advisory boards of two professional journals, has spoken at more than a hundred business conferences, and lectured in various universities worldwide. He has published several book chapters, edited a book on strategy and technology, and written articles in peer-reviewed as well as business journals. He has been interviewed and quoted extensively on television and in global publications, including the *Economist*, as an expert on the evolution of organizations. He is frequently sought out by national media in mature or rapidly developing economies to explain the implications of his work for their own companies.

Yves holds a PhD in industrial marketing from the University of Strathclyde in Scotland and a DEA in decision analysis and organizational sociology from the Paris Institute of Political Science (Sciences Po). He also attended the Scottish Business School, SKEMA Business School, and the Salzburg Seminar in American Studies. He lives in the Washington, DC, area.

Peter Tollman is a Boston-based senior partner and managing director at The Boston Consulting Group, which he joined in 1989. He leads BCG's People and Organization practice in North America. Prior leadership roles have included global leadership of BCG's Biopharmaceuticals sector and its R&D topic. He holds a PhD in engineering from the University of Cape Town, South Africa, and an MBA with distinction from Columbia Business School. Peter is an invited speaker at many company and industry conferences, and has authored a number of works on leadership, organization, and corporate performance.

As one of BCG's most experienced client-service partners, Peter has helped many of the world's leading corporations improve the competitiveness and performance of their organizations. His work has spanned the globe and involved a wide range of assignments, including organization restructurings, governance redesigns, culture change, workforce engagement, shareholder value and growth-enhancement initiatives, improvements to operational effectiveness and key processes, postmerger integrations, enterprisewide transformations, and guidance of CEOs and other senior leaders through leadership transitions.

He has helped clients gain insight from and successfully apply the simple rules across many of these efforts.

In addition to his BCG work, Peter was a founding managing director of MPM Capital, a healthcare venture capital company. He sits on the board of governors of the Jerusalem Academy of Music and Dance at the Hebrew University and is a trustee of Walnut Hill School for the Arts. Peter lives in the Boston area with his wife, Linda Kaplan, MD, and their two college-age daughters, Jessica and Sarah.